THE WILD-FLOWER GARDEN

THE
WILD-FLOWER
GARDEN

ROY GENDERS

DAVID & CHARLES

NEWTON ABBOT   LONDON

VANCOUVER

ISBN 0 7153 7154 1

Set in 12 on 13pt Bembo
and printed in Great Britain
by Latimer Trend & Company Ltd Plymouth
for David & Charles (Publishers) Limited
Brunel House   Newton Abbot   Devon

Published in Canada
by Douglas David & Charles Limited
1875 Welch Street   North Vancouver   BC

CONTENTS

1	Our Disappearing Flora	*page* 7
2	Wild Flowers and Their Uses in the Garden	12
3	A Wild-Flower Border	21
4	Wild Flowers for Small Beds	37
5	Wild Flowers for Wall and Paving	47
6	A Wild-Flower Rock Garden	61
7	Wild Flowers for the Water Garden	69
8	Dell and Spinney	82
9	Plants for the Shrub Garden	97
10	The Herb Garden	112
11	Propagating Wild Flowers	123
	Appendix A Wild Flowers and Their Common Names	130
	Appendix B The Wild-Flower Calendar	135
	Glossary	147
	Acknowledgements	149
	Index	151

1

OUR DISAPPEARING FLORA

They gathered flowers to fill their basket,
And with fine fingers cropped full feateously
The tender stalks on high.
Of every sort which in that meadow grew,
They gathered some; the violet, pallid blue,
The little daisy that at evening closes,
The virgin lily, and the primrose true . . .

Edmund Spenser

In Spenser's Elizabethan England wild flowers were plentiful everywhere and there was no harm in gathering blooms to enjoy at home
as each appeared in its season. Today, however, these same flowers are
disappearing so fast that even picking them should not be con-
doned.

Cutting into the limestone cliffs of north-east Yorkshire is a ravine
which runs down to the sea, and here can be found a greater number of
wild flowers than I have ever seen growing together elsewhere.
During the winter these plants are constantly lashed by north-
easterly gales and covered by spray from the sea. Yet each year, from
early spring until almost the year's end, they flower in their simple
beauty, and by midsummer the ravine is as colourful as a long-
established herbaceous border in an old cottage garden. Here can be
found the common St John's wort and sweet amber, the bladder
campion, the night-flowering catchfly, the yellow wallflower, violets
and cowslips, herb Robert and the musk stork's-bill, salad burnet and
common agrimony, herb bennet, rose root and at least a hundred
others. Many are scented and, long before the ravine is reached, their
soft perfume can be detected in the gentle breezes that blow from the
sea. It is a flower-lover's paradise, and few like it remain.

Such plants should not be dug up and removed from the countryside, for our wild flowers are all too rapidly disappearing. This is due to many causes, not least of which is the rapid suburban spread in recent years, when much of the land preserved around our large towns, for the enjoyment of the citizens as 'green belt' areas, has come to be used for building. There has also been widespread depletion of many deciduous woodlands for the acquisition of their timber, and many of these have not been replanted. The many miles of new motorways has meant the destruction of much of our countryside, and, for its part, large-scale farming and the use of the combine harvester has brought about the removal of miles of hedgerow beneath which once grew many of our loveliest plants. In the last thirty years it is believed that more than 150,000 miles of hedges have been removed, leaving only those which play a part in agricultural activity in their function as a windbreak. Thus the continuity of woodland and hedgerow has gone, and with it the spread of our wild flowers from woodland to hedgerow and from one field to the next. On many farms, where there was once a thick hedge sheltering countless wild flowers, and supporting much wildlife, providing nectar for bees and butterflies, berries, insects and nesting sites for birds, cover for the dormouse, and food and protection for other creatures, there is now open country, made profitable by the plough, but only at the expense of much of the flora and fauna of our islands. As the insects leave, so the flowers lose their pollinators and then they, too, eventually cease to exist. A hedge is the most valuable sanctuary for wildlife and plants, for here they are given shelter from the heat of the mid-day sun, and find moisture in summer and food throughout the year. The hedge offers protection from draughts and cold winds, and provides humus for plants in that each year, as the leaves fall, the depth of soil increases as they decompose, thus retaining moisture in dry weather whilst providing plantlife with additional nourishment.

It is not general knowledge that most plants, of which the cowslip and primrose are but two examples, tend to form their new roots from the crown, at a point just beneath the surface of the soil thus tending to push the plant upwards, exposing the new roots to hot sunshine and drying winds. As there is now little over-crowding, and consequent shelter, these old-fashioned flowers in modern gardens do not flourish as they did in the old cottage gardens where they sheltered each other from the hot summer sunlight and protected each other

1 Cheddar pink

from cold winds. In addition, each plant was given an almost continuous supply of mulching materials at the crown. This came from the decaying foliage of nearby plants and the liberal spreading of manure and clearings from ditches. Each year, the newly formed roots were provided with the nourishment they needed to maintain their vigour. The situation is exactly the same with our wild flowers, so many of which have been deprived of humus and moisture as hedgerows and woodlands have been removed. But a hedge, whether in garden or farm, requires attention in trimming and layering, and every few years new branches must be partially cut and bent over to fill in the gaps. These shoots are inter-woven between stakes driven into the ground at regular intervals, and it becomes a costly business to maintain a truly efficient hedge. More and more, therefore, are likely to be removed.

Again, cutting grass verges along the roadsides also demands expensive labour, and, on busy roads, unkept hedges and verges become a danger to motorists, obscuring their view. County councils have, therefore, had to make more and more use of herbicides resulting in the indiscriminate destruction of countless wild flowers, many of which, like dandelion, thistle and groundsel, provide the seeds our birds depend upon for food.

The preservation of wild flowers in gardens will not only bring the beauty of the countryside to the town and be a means of preserving our national flora, but may also help to preserve our wildlife. Butterflies and bees, now finding it more and more difficult to obtain suitable food plants will come into the garden, whilst birds can feed upon the seeds of many plants if these are not cut back after flowering until the year's end.

Almost all our wild flowers are readily raised from seed and are, of course, completely suited to the climate and soil conditions of our islands. Whilst there must be no attempt to dig up wild flowers, and even careless picking of the blooms may cause serious damage to the plants, it may be possible to collect the seeds of many which will have ripened during a dry summer. Cowslip and forget-me-not, mullein and foxglove, elecampane and cornflower set seed in abundance, and the seed pods may be removed with a sharp pair of scissors, causing no damage to the plants. The pods should be placed in envelopes or small boxes and spread out in an airy room to dry fully before being placed in cellophane envelopes and clearly named. They will then be ready to sow in spring. (Homegrown seed may be obtained in the same way.) It is, however, preferable to obtain seed only from annual and biennial plants which die after flowering, for perennials growing in the garden are seriously weakened if allowed to set seed, though cowslips and primroses may be allowed to retain one or two flowers on each established plant to form seed, the others being removed as soon as they die back. Most perennials are better increased by offsets, or by root division.

More than twenty of our rarest wild flowers are now protected by the Wild Creatures and Wild Plants Protection Act, introduced in Parliament by Mr P. Hardy, MP for Rother Valley, and made law in 1975. Under this, the Cheddar pink, blue heath, lady's slipper and military orchids and the Snowdon lily are protected, with a

2   Lady's slipper orchid

fine of £100 liable for the uprooting of any of them. However, no wild-flower plants should be removed from the countryside however plentiful they are, for they can all be obtained from specialist growers who have held stocks for many years, whilst others, easily raised from seed, are also obtainable from specialist seedsmen, if one cannot obtain one's own seed direct from the countryside.

All who possess a garden, however small, whether in town or country, should include in it at least a few of the fast-disappearing flowers of the countryside—even if only those like the salad burnet, common marjoram and chicory which are grown purely for their culinary uses—for they are all delightful plants with a charm entirely their own. They can be set anywhere in the garden and will provide colour and interest throughout the year.

2

WILD FLOWERS AND THEIR USES IN THE GARDEN

> Flowers embody and express the season of the year
> that owns them. The sheeted blue in the clean woods
> of bluebell time, with white companies of wind
> flowers growing between, speak of the pale wide
> blue of new May skies with small white clouds scud-
> ding their perfection.
>
> Pamela Tennant, *Village Notes*

Besides their beauty in the garden, wild flowers have many uses today, just as they had for the countryman of long ago. The wood avens, *Geum urbanum*, has a root which, when dried, has an aromatic clove-like perfume, once used to improve the taste of beer. Today, the roots are more often used tied in small bundles and placed in an apple tart or pie before cooking, to impart a clove-like taste. Indeed, the plant takes its name from the Greek *geuo*, 'I taste', from which it would seem these roots were appreciated in cooking during early times.

Surprisingly, wood avens is a plant of the rose family, as is the lovely common agrimony and the fragrant agrimony with its sweetly resinous leaves. These are delightful slender perennials, growing 2ft tall, with yellow flowers borne in spire-like racemes. Whilst the former species is common everywhere, the fragrant agrimony is now present only in south-west England and South Wales. Both flowers and leaves retain their aromatic fragrance, in the same way as walnut leaves, so that, long after drying, they could be used in making pot pourris and for stuffing pillows and cushions, often accompanied by hops to encourage sleep. The leaves were also in demand for making a tonic beer. Salad burnet is just as interesting.

The insignificant greenish-brown flowers (like those of thrift) could not recommend this plant for garden display, but its ladder-like leaves, dark green in colour, act as a pleasing foil to other plants with brightly coloured flowers, and are delicious when used in a salad, imparting a mild cucumber flavour. They are also pleasant with cream cheese in a sandwich, as are cowslip leaves, although only one or two should be removed from the plant each springtime, otherwise it will lose vigour.

One of the most interesting of the early Elizabethan writers, Gerard, mentions finding wild flowers in all manner of places around London. He found lily-of-the-valley in Kenwood, woodruff in Gray's Inn Lane, bugloss in the dry ditches of Piccadilly, whilst 'sweet rocket', he said, was to be found 'as you go from Lambeth Bridge to the village of Lambeth, under a small bridge that you must pass over hard by Thames-side'. He describes it as being 'a good salad herb if it be eaten with lettuce, purslane, and such cold herbs'.

It is surprising how many of our wild flowers could be eaten in salads and soups. The violet and primrose, for instance, may be used in salad, adding to its appearance as well as taste, and there are other flowers which have for long been used by the countryman to improve his meat diet. Few would have thought that the leaves of sweet rocket were edible, but the plant is a member of the cabbage family and the leaves, which are slightly bitter, do improve a salad. Though possibly not a native plant, it became naturalised (like the wallflower) at an

3   Sweet rocket

early date in our history and is one of the loveliest of wild flowers. So, too, is lady's smock, a plant of watermeadows which Shakespeare mentioned and which he must often have seen along the banks of the Avon. At a distance, the flowers take on the metallic-mauve appearance of polished silver. In Shakespeare's time, its leaves were used in early summer salads in place of lettuce and they have the bitter, pungent taste of watercress which is usually found growing nearby, at the water's edge. Lady's smock leaves contain similar vitamins and mineral salts to watercress which, after all, is of the same *Cruciferae* family. The leaves are as delicious as those of borage when placed with cheese in sandwiches.

One of the loveliest of all plants in bloom, borage is an annual or biennial, growing 2–3ft tall and bearing, in forked cymes, brilliant blue flowers with jet black anthers. The flowers are not scented, but when the leaves are broken they release a pleasant cucumber-like smell which so improves the flavour of cider and Pimm's No 1, making a cool, sustaining drink, that the leaves are used in the best hotels. In the *Proper New Boke of Cookery*, written and published anonymously during Elizabethan times, there is a recipe for borage tart which I have tried and found most satisfying.

Take borage flowers and parboil until tender. Strain away surplus moisture and whip in the yolk of three eggs, together with some boiled apple. Cover pastry with the mixture and bake until nicely browned.

The leaves fried in batter, make delicious fritters, especially when covered with hot cheese sauce, and both leaves and flowers can be used fresh in salads. Placed with cream cheese in sandwiches, the leaves also made a nourishing mid-day meal for ploughmen to enjoy with their cider or beer.

Writing in *Herbal Simples* at the turn of the century, Dr Fernie, a Glasgow physician, said that the reputed powers of invigoration after eating borage leaves could be medically substantiated, for the juice contained 30 per cent nitrate of potash. John Pechey, whose *English Herbal of Physical Plants* was published in 1694, included borage as one of the four most important cordial flowers and said, 'the distilled water comfort the heart, relieve the faint, cheer the melancholy, and purify the blood'. In the household book of the fifth earl of Northumberland, for 1502, there is a list of plants 'to stylle' for making cordial

4　Chicory

waters, included amongst which are borage, columbine, bugloss,
sorrel, cowslip, scabious, tansy, wormwood, dandelion and hart's-
tongue (fern), all of them amongst the loveliest of wild flowers to
grow in a garden.

In his *Five Hundred Points of Good Husbandry*, published in 1573,
Thomas Tusser, an Essex man born at Rivenhall, included amongst
his 'flowers to styll', the lovely chicory, its flower being the bluest of
all blue flowers, without a trace of purple. A perennial, it was at one
time seen by the wayside everywhere. Now it is becoming scarce, yet
is one of the most valuable plants to have in a garden. The forced
roots make a most appetising winter vegetable, whilst the leaves,
when included in soups, are nourishing and easily digested to help
sustain those who are weak after long illness. Like so many wild
flowers, its blooms provide a distilled water which gives a sparkle
when tired eyes are bathed with it, whilst an infusion of the whole
plant in hot water will, if applied at bedtime, clear the skin of
blemishes. It was one of the countrywoman's most sought-after
cosmetics during the time when she relied entirely upon the flowers
and leaves of those plants growing wild in her garden and the surrounding countryside. The distilled water of the marshmallow was
also a valuable skin tonic, as was that made from lily-of-the-valley
flowers—the most prized of all skin tonics used by the women of
ancient Greece and Rome.

From chamomile flowers a tea was made to soothe tired nerves and the same preparation also used as a hair tonic, as was the distilled water of the handsome mullein, a biennial which should be found in every border. Until quite recent times it was grown in every cottage garden for its many uses. Cottagers would dry the stems and thick flannel-like leaves, and make them into tallow which would burn for hours with an iridescent light, hence the plant's names of candlewick and hedge taper. The thick woolly leaves were put into children's shoes when the soles were wearing thin, to protect the feet from rough, gravelly roads. The plant takes its name from the French *mol*, meaning 'soft'. Best of all its many uses, it was the countryman's standby for the relief of ear-ache. The fresh flowers were steeped in olive oil for three weeks, left in a sunny window, then strained. Two or three drops in the ear would quickly ease a pain and a few drops taken in warm water before bedtime cured children of bed-wetting.

Several of our wild flowers, including tansy, lady's smock, common agrimony and fennel, were in demand as blood purifiers, whilst tonic beers were made from each of these plants in addition to that from chamomile, borage and chicory. Pleasant summer drinks were made from cowslip, marshmallow, peppermint, pennyroyal and from alkanet, which John Evelyn said possessed qualities similar to borage, so that its flowers and leaves could be eaten in salads and placed in summer drinks.

The stately elecampane, our largest wild flower, and St John's wort also, had many uses and they, too, should be in every garden if only for their beauty. Elecampane is found near old castles and was at one time common by the wayside and in woodlands south of the Thames, although it has now become quite rare. Of this plant, William Coles said: 'It is one of those plants whereof England may boast as much as any for there grows none better in the world than in England.' Coles published his *Art of Simpling* in 1656 when the plant was much in demand for the relief of a hard cough and for asthmatical complaints, although it was the root that was used. These were also candied, like those of the sea holly, and eaten as sweetmeats as an aid to the digestion. Pliny the Elder, who perished at Pompeii, said that 'Julia Augusta let no day pass without eating some of the roots of ennula, candied'. The roots which have the scent of violets when dry, also release a sweet violet perfume when burnt slowly on a low fire or on

Plate 1 Anne Hathaway's cottage as seen from the orchard. In the garden the author found daffodils, cowslips, violets, wood anemones, columbines, cuckoo pint, herb Robert, primroses and wild thyme – all wild flowers mentioned by Shakespeare

Plate 2 Borage, *Borago officinalis*. Viewed against the light, the hairy stems have a luminous appearance, above which gleams the intense sky blue of the star-like blooms.

Plate 3 The chequered daffodil or snakeshead lily, *Fritillaria meleagris*

embers, and for this reason were often used to fumigate a musty room in the days of earthen floors covered with rushes.

For the same reason, houses were strewn with fragrant native flowers and leaves. It was not until early Tudor times, when overseas trade was expanded, that plants were introduced from abroad. Until the end of the sixteenth century, flowers and leaves were used in large quantities for strewing, and one of the charges of extravagance brought against Cardinal Wolsey by Henry VIII was that he ordered the floors of his palace of Hampton Court to be covered all too often with sweet-scented rushes. These were the stems and leaves of *Acorus calamus*, the sweet flag, which grows mostly in the fenlands of Norfolk and Cambridgeshire and in the marshy lands of northern Europe, and so were obtained at great cost. It is a plant to be used at the side of a garden pool, together with those other lovely wild flowers, the marsh marigold and forget-me-not which also prefer damp places.

Tusser gave us a list of those wild flowers most commonly used for strewing the floors of manor house, cottage and the church pew. In it appear cowslip and fennel, tansy and chamomile, costmary and penny-royal. One surprising omission is that handsome plant, the meadow-sweet, which Queen Elizabeth enjoyed above all others to have on the floors of her apartments. Gerard, who looked after Lord Burghley's gardens in Strand and had his own apothecary's garden where Fetter Lane is now, said that 'meadowsweet far excells all other strewing herbs to deck up houses, to strew in chambers, halls and banqueting rooms in summertime, for the smell thereof [when walked upon] makes the heart merry and joyful and delighteth the senses'. A hundred years later, fine quality rugs and carpets began to arrive from the Near East and wild flowers were no longer in demand for strewing.

Scented waters made from wild flowers were also used to relieve the musty smell of rooms, and in the days before dry cleaning were sprinkled over one's clothes. A cheap rose-scented water may be made from the roots of *Sedum roseum*, the rose-root of cottage gardens, which Gerard tells of finding on Ingleborough Fells, 'from whence I have had plants for my garden', he wrote. Then it was to be found in stony places everywhere and little harm would be done by Gerard lifting a few roots to plant in his Holborn garden, though today the plant is rare in the wild.

B

So many of our wild flowers are useful in so many ways apart from ornamentation. That they are now so neglected as garden plants is due mostly to the fact that for many years their place has been taken by those of more brilliant colouring which have reached us from distant climes, and to their being always readily available in the countryside; they were there for the taking. But this is no longer so. Many are dying out, many, not protected, are becoming scarcer each year and their beauty may now be enjoyed only when grown in a garden. In addition, as shown, they may be used for food and for simple remedies, for natural beauty treatment and to make sweet waters and pot pourris. They are indeed plants for all purposes.

3

A WILD-FLOWER BORDER

I love flowers; not for a young girl's reason,
But because these brief visitors to us
Rise yearly from the neighbourhood of the dead,
To show us how far fairer and more lovely
Their world is.

Thomas Lovell Beddoes, *Flowers*

A border planted with wild flowers can be entirely as satisfying as one planted with those from foreign lands which, for so many years, have enjoyed the attentions of the hybridist. These may have greater brilliance and a more compact habit, for these are qualities that have been bred into them. They are perhaps more easily grouped about a border and maintained with the minimum of attention, yet they lack the simple charm and informality of our own wild flowers which blend with each other in the border just as in their natural surroundings. They are entirely at home in a garden and will become fully perennial if the soil is well drained in winter and in a friable condition at the time of planting.

As several of the hardy border plants will be tall growing, if possible select a position where they will not be subjected to strong winds. Ideally, a border should be made with an old wall as a background, on the side of the garden which stands against the prevailing winds. It may even be possible to make the border in the lee of a house or outhouse. Again, a windbreak can be made by erecting interwoven fencing around that part of the garden selected for the border. A trellis, made with builder's laths and treated with a wood preservative, about which native honeysuckle and traveller's joy are allowed to climb, may be erected where it will divide part of the garden, to make one garden within another, entered through a small opening in the trellis, over which an archway will give a pleasing effect. This inner garden can be made at the end of the garden of a semi-detached house, taking in the entire width, but in depth requiring no more than 8ft, with a bed down each side joined by a longer border on the side opposite the trellis. Interwoven fencing may be erected on three sides to give privacy and shelter.

A garden seat can be placed just inside the trellis, preferably on flagstones so that the ground will remain clean in wet weather. Surrounded by the stones and borders could be a lawn possibly with a stone sundial or birdbath at the centre. The scene will be further enhanced by the planting of several native hedgerow trees at the back of the border. (Four or five maximum, otherwise they will deprive the plants of sunlight as they begin to spread out.) For this purpose, I suggest the white and pink-flowering May which is especially attractive in standard form, *Crataegus alba plena* and *C rosea plena*, both having double flowers. The flowering crab, *Malus floribunda* with its graceful arching stems wreathed in pale pink blossom is also a delight during April and May. The native bird cherry, which flourishes in a cold climate in heavy soil, is an interesting small tree, its fragrant white blossom borne in elegant sprays during June. A better form is *Prunus padus rhexii*, which has delightful double flowers, like tiny rosettes of finest white which dangle on 2in footstalks, whilst purple queen has dark purple tinted foliage. The bird cherries grow no more than 10ft tall and in half-standard form make spreading heads. *P padus rhexii* holds its petals for several weeks, after which they litter the ground in a snow-white carpet of confetti.

Making the Border

To prepare a border, begin at the back and work forward. Dig to the depth of a spade (a 'spit' is the gardening term), clearing the soil of all perennial weeds and working-in whatever humus materials are available. These may consist of clearings from ditches if you live in the country, or straw dampened and composted with an activator, which may be obtained from any garden shop or seedsman. Decayed cow or farmyard manure is valuable, as is peat and used hops. Those living in the industrial north will be able to obtain wool or cotton shoddy quite inexpensively, while those near the coast may use chopped seaweed. Humus, which opens up winter soil to let the rains drain away, and retains moisture in summer, is more important than large quantities of manure which will cause the plants to make excess leaf at the expense of bloom. Wild flowers require humus, rather than manure, and will respond to a yearly top dressing of whatever materials are available by remaining healthy for many years. The humus should be worked right up to the crown of the plant and will supply the new roots with moisture and nourishment.

The ground is prepared, if possible, during November and the soil left in a rough state for the frosts and winds of winter to pulverise. For a heavy soil, work in some grit or boiler ash and perhaps some mortar or crushed brick from old buildings. If a quantity of caustic (unhydrated) lime (obtainable from a builder's merchant) is dug in, this will break up the clay particles when it comes in contact with moisture in the soil, the lime disintegrating with an eruptive action. It will also sweeten the acid soil of a town garden.

The plants, which will have been raised from seed sown in the spring of the previous year or propagated either by root division or from cuttings (see Chapter 11), should be set out in the border in March, one year after sowing seed. The plants will have wintered in a bed sheltered from cold winds, or in boxes, possibly kept in a cold frame or in the shelter of wooden boards erected on the side of the prevailing wind. Do not plant when the soil is wet or may have frost still in it. Wait until it is friable and then plant after first raking down the surface.

It is advisable first to make a plan of the position of the plants so that they may be correctly grouped as to their heights and distances apart, otherwise plants of taller habit may be set in the middle of the border, whilst those of bushy habit may be planted too close together. Grouping should be done so that the plants will be seen to best advantage, with the taller at the back, those of medium height at the centre and those of most compact habit to the front. If perennials are used, most of them will be permanent and when, after four or five years, the border has become overcrowded, some may be lifted, divided and replanted and the soil enriched as work continues during March and April. Spring planting is to be preferred for then the plants can get away to a good start and will not have their roots standing in the cold winter soil whilst they are inactive, often resulting in the plants damping-off in a winter of excessive rainfall.

When planting, use a broad-nose trowel so that the hole can be made large enough to take all the roots which are spread well out. Cover with soil and tread in firmly, and then insert a wooden label with the name of each plant.

A more pleasing effect will be obtained if planting is done in small groups of three or four so that the full beauty of the blooms is seen to advantage. Many plants will need to be used in the wild-flower border to make each group as colourful as possible. Planting will be easier if the border is first marked out with circles of sand to coincide with the arrangement of the plants on the planning chart, and each area marked with a label showing the name of the plant. This will save much time when planting.

Back-row Plants

For the back of the border, plant the common mullein, *Verbascum thapsus*. Although a biennial, there is no other suitable place in the garden to have it and, in a friable loam, it will reach a height of 6ft in a single summer. With its thick woolly leaves and towering flower spike, composed of multitudes of small yellow flowers with orange anthers, it never fails to attract attention. If the spike is left on until late autumn, and the ground around is undisturbed, it will seed itself each year. The flower spike remains colourful from early July until October.

Almost as tall growing is another of our lovely native flowers, the giant bellflower or rocket, *Campanula latifolia*. Its unbranched stems reaching a height of 4–5ft, it blooms over the same period as the mullein. It is widespread in sheltered woodlands in the north and in Ireland, has lanceolate leaves and bears large blue bell-shaped flowers 2in across, twenty or more appearing on each spike with the lower flowers opening first. The rare rampion, *C rapunculus*, more common in the south, grows 2ft tall and bears unbranched spikes of violet flowers. A water distilled from the leaves used to be considered excellent for the complexion.

Elecampane makes a majestic back-of-the-border plant, bearing, in July and August, the largest flower of all our native plants, like a small sunflower. Now rare, it is found occasionally in copses and hedge-rows, growing to a height of 4–5ft, with deeply crinkled and downy leaves 12in long, whilst the golden-rayed flowers measure more than

5 Sea holly

3in across. The most interesting part of the plant, however, is its root which Gerard said is 'as thick as a man may grip, blackish without, white within, . . . sweet of smell'. When first dug up, the root smells strongly of ripe bananas, then, as it dries, it takes on a violet scent which is retained after slicing and candying. Elecampane cakes were once sold as a sweetmeat, eaten to sweeten the breath, and were kept in stock by most of London's apothecaries.

Another favourite sweetmeat was the eringoe, the candied root of the sea holly, *Eryngium maritimum*, so popular during Elizabethan times and mentioned by Falstaff in *The Merry Wives of Windsor*:

> Let the sky rain potatoes; let it thunder to the
> tune of Greensleeves; hail kissing comfits; and
> snow eringoes . . .

An erect perennial, growing 3ft tall with spiny leaves like those of holly, and sky-blue flowers with spiny bracts, it is common around the shores of Kent and Essex, usually growing in sand and shingle. In the garden it requires a well-drained sandy soil for the roots extend far down, like parsnips. At one time they were used in the same way, boiled and served with a sauce as an accompaniment to meat.

The common mallow, *Malva sylvestris* is a handsome back-of-the-border plant but will often seed itself about the rest of the garden where it becomes a nuisance. If not removed when small, the roots will penetrate to a great depth and become so tough as to make their removal most difficult. It also sprawls out to cover a large area with its ivy-like leaves. For all that it is a beautiful plant, growing 3–4ft tall and bearing its mauve-pink cup-shaped flowers from June until October when bees will take the nectar and the almost pure-white pollen.

The musk mallow, which grows to half this height, has narrowly cut divided leaves, whilst the flowers are larger, being 2in across and of a deeper mauve-pink. The flowers of all the mallows are self-pollinating and are not in any way scented, but the stems and leaves of the musk mallow, which are covered in hairs, emit a musk-like smell when handled, like that of the musk storksbill and the so-called musk plant (*Mimulus*) of cottage gardens which later lost its hairs and, with them, its perfume. The *Malva* was so named by Linnaeus, from a Greek word meaning 'soft', in reference to the hairy characteristics of the stem and leaf, giving it a silky feel.

Motherwort, *Leonurus cardiaca*, is a tall-growing labiate, reaching a height of 4ft in loamy soil with the lower leaves deeply cut into segments, whilst the pale mauve flowers are borne in whorls from the axils of the leaves from July until September. It was once widespread about our hedgerows, but is rapidly becoming less prevalent. A popular plant with countrymen, a syrup was made by boiling the leaves with honey and taken to relieve palpitation of the heart, hence its botanical name.

Another back-row plant is the hemp agrimony, *Eupatorium cannabinum*, also known as water agrimony because it grows in damp places. However, provided it is given a moisture-holding soil, it will grow perfectly well in a border. It has attractive hemp-like leaves

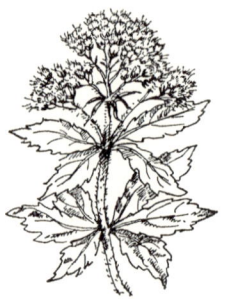

6 Hemp agrimony

and bears its pale lilac flowers in terminal cymes from July until September. Its aromatic leaves contain tannin and a decoction from these may be gargled to ease a sore throat.

A showy plant for the back of a border is the rosebay or willow herb, *Epilobium angustifolium*, a perennial growing 3-4ft tall, with dark green narrow willow-like leaves and bearing, from June until October, tapering spikes of bright rose-purple flowers. One of the most conspicuous of our wild flowers it prefers its own company and so is often seen on land cleared of timber, or on a fire-blackened moorland, hence its country name of fireweed. It is a plant much visited by bees and the resulting honey is the palest of all with a distinctive flavour. Though colourful in the border, because this plant increases by underground stems, it often becomes a troublesome weed, whilst its fluffy seed heads give it a somewhat untidy appearance.

Mid-border Plants

The Canterbury bell, *Campanula medium*, although biennial, is at its loveliest only in a large border for it grows 18-24in tall and makes a dense bushy plant, its huge bells of blue, pink or white presenting a rich display during June. Though it is said that the plant is not native to Britain, all the early garden writers mention it growing wild. Gerard tells us that 'it do growe pentifully in the lowe woods and hedgerows of Kent, about Canterbury, Sittingborne, Southfleet and Greenhythe'. It takes its name from the bells of Canterbury Cathedral and was used as their symbol by Chaucer's pilgrims.

This plant is for the middle of the border and will, with its bushy habit, hide the sparse lower stems of many of the taller back-row plants. After flowering, it may be noticed that another rosette of bright green leaves has formed at the base alongside the old spike. In this case, cut away the old spike near ground level for the new rosette will bear a flower spike the following year.

The hound's tongue, *Cynoglossum officinale*, is one of the loveliest of border plants, growing 2ft tall, with broad grey-green lanceolate leaves, like a hound's tongue in shape. It bears its maroon-coloured flowers from June until September when they give way to spiny fruits which cling to one's clothes.

The common sea lavender, *Limonium vulgare* (not in any way connected with the labiates, but of the maritime thrift family), may readily be raised from seed. A perennial, growing 15–18in tall, it too requires a sandy soil. It blooms from July until September, bearing flat-topped clusters of lavender-mauve flowers above a rosette of leaves. The flowers produce large amounts of nectar and are frequently worked by bees as an alternative to heather.

The soapwort, *Saponaria officinalis*, is a pleasing perennial for the border, especially in its double form, the flesh-pink flowers being, in the words of old Sir Thomas Hanmer, 'fulsomely sweet'. There is also a double white form, *alba plena*, the whiteness of the flowers being accentuated by the dark green foliage. Both the leaves and stems when crushed yield a milky liquid, saponin, which monks once used as soap, for it lathers well when mixed with water. Parkinson, who published his famous *Paradisus in Sole* in 1629 and dedicated it to Charles I's queen, called the plant bouncing Bet, for it tends to creep about, rooting at the leaf nodes. The bruised leaves act as an antiseptic and could be rubbed into cuts or bound over sores.

Another delightful plant, especially in its double form, is lady's smock, *Cardamine pratensis*. As it grows about 18in tall, it should be planted to the front of a border where it will bloom from early May until mid-July, its mauve flowers having a silvered appearance. The plant was dedicated to Our Lady for it is in bloom at Lady-tide. It was also called cuckoo flower for its bloom coincides with the arrival of the cuckoo. It is a plant of damp meadows, and requires a moisture-retentive soil. Of the same family as watercress, the leaves have the same bitterness and are equally pleasant in a salad. They are packed with iron salts and vitamins. The plant was also considered to be a

7 Soapwort

8 Lady's smock

cure for epilepsy, twelve grains of the dried and powdered flowers being taken three times a day.

The wild peony, *Paeonia corallina*, grows to about the same height. It is one of the rarest plants of the British Isles, found only on the rocky islet of Steep Holm in the Bristol Channel, where it may have been introduced during medieval times and is now a protected plant. It has great beauty, with glossy dark green leaves and bearing, in May, a large flower of rich crimson-red, more than 4in across, with prominent stamens tipped with gold. It was so named because of its coral-red seeds which were used to flavour meats.

This plant is also known as *P mascula*, the male peony, whilst *P officinalis* is the female peony. In its double form the latter came to be grown in English gardens as the double red and double pink peony. They have no perfume and it was not until the arrival of *P lactiflora*, towards the end of the nineteenth century, that perfume came to be bred into the modern hybrids. This plant had been discovered in the Siberian wastes by a Russian traveller, its roots being cooked, like potatoes, and eaten by the Mongols. Both the male and female peonies are almost indestructible if planted in a deep, moist soil and will remain vigorous for fifty years or more. Plant in the late autumn, when the roots are dormant, about 2ft apart. All they require is an annual top dressing of decayed manure, during November.

The common agrimony, *Agrimonia eupatoria*, is one of the loveliest of wild flowers, growing no more than 2ft tall and bearing its small yellow flowers in graceful spiked racemes. Both flowers and roots have the delicious fruity scent of ripe apricots. A common plant of hedgerows and pastures, it blooms during July and August, and to the countryman was one of the most useful of all plants. It was included in the *London Pharmacopaea*, and John Pechey advised those afflicted with jaundice to drink ale in which the leaves had been infused.

A delicious tonic wine can be made by boiling two handfuls of the flowers, for 20 minutes, with 4oz of ginger. Pour into a large jug containing 2 sliced lemons, 4 sliced oranges and 4lb of sugar. Allow to stand for 3 days, then strain into a large earthenware jar and allow to ferment. It will be ready to use in 6 months' time, a wineglassful daily being both pleasant and beneficial

The yarrow, *Achillea millefolium*, is always a popular middle-of-the-border plant, growing 18–20in tall, with its dark green leaflets finely cut into segments, and white or pink flowers borne in flat terminal cymes. It is mostly found on grassy banks and mountainous slopes, but in the garden grows well in all soils, flowering from early June until September. The improved forms, fire king, crimson and cerise queen are outstanding garden plants, and if cut when at their best and hung upside down in a cool, airy room for a month, they may be used in longlasting flower arrangements and will retain their beauty until Christmas.

The plant was known to the Greeks as *liera*, 'holy herb', for if the leaves were bound against open wounds they would stem the flow of blood; or else a decoction of the leaves might be poured over wounds before binding. Carpenters kept a bottle always at hand, and for this reason it came to be called carpenter's weed.

A ptarmica, the sneezewort, so called, Turner said 'because the flowers make one sneeze exceedingly', is a delightful border plant, especially in the double form, *flore plena* which countrymen knew as 'shirt buttons'. Found in dry meadows and heaths, it blooms in June and July, and brides would often include the flowers in their bouquets. From the leaves a 'tea' was brewed, with a taste like 'catmint tea', and, dried and powdered, the leaves were mixed with those of chamomile and inhaled as snuff. The plant grows 2ft tall and, when cut and in water, the flowers will last for several weeks. A garden variety known as the pearl is outstanding in its freedom of flowering and in the quality of its bloom. The plant is distinguished from the yarrow, when not in bloom, by its undivided but serrated leaves.

9 Wood betony

Another delightful mid-border plant is wood betony, *Stachys betonica* (syn *Betonica officinalis*), a hairy perennial growing 12–15in tall and often present in damp woodlands. The rich rosy-purple flowers are frequented by bees during July and August and the leaves are so densely haired as to appear greyish-white. Gerard believed that eating betony leaves stimulated the appetite, whilst the fresh leaves, placed on the forehead and covered with a damp cloth, would relieve the most tiresome headache.

Dame's violet or sweet rocket, *Hesperis matronalis*, growing 3ft tall, is for planting near the middle of the border. A native of southern Europe, it has been naturalised on waste ground and in woodlands since earliest times, its purple or white flowers, borne in loose racemes being scented of violets in the evening. It is often seen growing against old walls, and was so popular during Elizabethan times that it was known as queen's gillyflowers. It is readily raised from seed sown in April, transplanting the seedlings 15in apart.

The sweet or field scabious, *Scabiosa arvensis*, could accompany it in the middle of the border for it grows to a similar height. This blooms from July until the end of summer, having flowers of soft lilac-mauve with tightly packed florets, resembling pin cushions. They have a delicious perfume and are much visited by butterflies and bees. The plants are raised from seed sown in April, in boxes placed in a frame or covered with glass. Transplant 12in apart. This is a long-lasting flower when cut and placed in water, and does not drop its petals.

Front-row Plants

For the front of the border, Jacob's ladder, *Polemonium coeruleum*, is a dainty little plant with ladder-like leaflets, and bearing, in June and July, open spikes filled with masses of tiny blue flowers on 18in stems. In the wild, it is confined to the limestone outcrops of northern England but has for long been a cottage-garden plant, for its brilliant sky-blue colouring attracts the bees which work it for its nectar and bright orange pollen.

The meadow cranesbill, *Geranium pratense*, a hardy perennial, is a suitable companion as it grows to a similar height and is in bloom at the same time, its bright blue flowers being held above deeply lobed leaves. Bees search for the nectar which is secreted at the base of the stamens, whilst its pollen grains are amongst the largest of any wild flowers.

Bees will also work the maroon-black flowers of G *phaeum*, the dusky cranesbill of dry banks and railway cuttings. These open during May and early June when blossom is often scarce, and the plant grows about 12in tall. Another charming plant, the bloody cranesbill, G *sanguineum*, which grows 9in tall and bears blood-red flowers, should be planted to the front of a border. It is also visited by bees and like the other species is usually found in the north, on limestone formations, growing with the more common and less interesting dovesfoot cranesbill, which bears pinkish-mauve flowers from April to September.

Clary, or clear eyes, *Salvia horminoides*, is a good front-of-the-

10   Meadow cranesbill

border perennial, needing a well-drained soil to be long living. It is in bloom from mid-June until September, and grows 12in tall, with hairy dark green leaves and flowers of deepest blue. Gerard said that he found it 'at the end of Chelsea, next to London; and in the highway as you go from the Queen's (Elizabeth I) Palace of Richmond to the water's side'. In other words, it was once prevalent in damp meadows south of the Thames but is now almost entirely a garden plant.

The French made a highly narcotic wine from its leaves, whilst countrymen used them in omelettes, and steeped the seeds in water to bathe the eyes. The dried and powdered root was also taken as snuff to ease a head cold and, with their pleasant smell, the leaves used to make sweet bags.

The closely related meadow sage, *S pratensis*, is equally attractive with its whorled spikes of purple-blue which reach a height of about 2ft. Its crinkled leaves are aromatic and are toothed at the edges so that the plant, which is present in hedgerows and by the side of woodlands, may easily be mistaken for clary. It blooms from June until August.

An excellent border plant, growing 18in tall, is bistort, *Polygonum bistorta*, especially the variety *supurbum* which bears pinkish-red spikes on 2ft stems throughout the summer. The bluish-green arrow-shaped leaves were at one time used in stuffings, whilst a water distilled from the roots will bring relief to sore gums if rubbed onto them. It is a plant of the North Country, present on hilly pastures.

Lungwort, *Pulmonaria officinalis*, is interesting, being present in hedgerows and woodlands mostly in the south. Parkinson said that it was discovered by John Goodier, 'a great searcher and lover of plants, dwelling at Maple-Durham in Hampshire'. A perennial, it grows about 10in tall. Its oval leaves are spotted with white and so it was named from the Latin *pulmo*, 'a lung', an example of the old Doctrine of Signatures in which plants associated with parts of the human body in appearance were thought capable of affecting a cure for their diseases. Countrymen would use the leaves in pottage, and boiled in poultices, to ease a tight chest. The flowers, which are coloured blue and pink, appear during April and May. The variety Bowle's Red bears bright reddish-pink flowers which turn blue as they fade.

Herb bennet, the blessed herb, also the wood avens, *Geum urbanum*, makes a colourful front-of-the-border plant, bearing a succession of neatly rounded golden-yellow flowers from June until September. It enjoys having shade about its roots, so is happy in the company of other border plants. The roots are the interesting part of this plant for, when dried, they emit a clove-like perfume and so were placed in clothes chests and those containing priests' vestments, not only to impart their fragrance but to keep away moths.

Culpeper, whose *Complete Herbal to Cure All Disorders Incident to Man*, first published in 1652, which became the countryman's standby for all remedies, mentions the clove-like fragrance of the roots when dry. During his time they were placed in ale to impart their warm flavour, and are also delicious baked in an apple pie or tart in place of cloves. A drink obtained from $\frac{1}{2}$oz of the dried and sliced root boiled in a pint of water and strained, will be conducive to sleep if a wine-glassful is taken at bedtime. The leaves also have the clove perfume but not as pronounced here as in the roots.

An appealing plant for near the front of the border is the vervain, *Verbena officinalis*. It is a square-stemmed hairy perennial, growing about 15in tall and bearing its pale mauve flowers in elegant spikes during the latter weeks of summer. It is not the lemon-scented verbena of the perfumer, for it is without scent, but an infusion of the leaves, sweetened with a little honey and drunk before bedtime, will ensure peaceful sleep and, when cool, will bring relief to tired eyes.

Here, too, plant the pink oxalis, *Oxalis floribunda*, once a favourite in every cottage garden. It makes a dense tuft of pale green shamrock-like leaves from which, on 6–8in stems, arise umbels of the bright rose-pink flowers which are produced from May until October. The plant enjoys a soil well enriched with humus.

The purple hawkweed, *Saussurea alpina*, is a suitable foil with its clusters of scented, deep purple flowers which appear from July until September on 10in stems. It is a plant of mountainous regions, mostly of the north and is enhanced by its dark green leaves.

The wild catmint, *Nepeta cataria*, grows to a similar height, and cat lovers should include it in their gardens, 'because', Gerard said, 'cats are very much delighted with it; for the smell of it is so pleasant to them that they rub themselves upon it and wallow and tumble in it and also feed on the leaves very greedily'.

Plate 4 Elecampane, *Inula helenium*

Plate 5 The Cheddar pink, *Dianthus gratianopolitanus*

Plate 6 Alpine pinks quickly establish themselves on a new rockery of red sandstone

4

WILD FLOWERS FOR SMALL BEDS

There is a flower I wish to wear
But not until first worn by you—
Heartease—of all Earth's flowers most rare!
Bring it; and bring enough for two.

Walter Savage Landor, *To Ianthe*

Many of those wild flowers, which are compact and dainty in their habit and enjoy a greater freedom of flowering than most cultivated plants, are most valuable for display in small garden beds. Such flowers possess extreme hardiness, are tolerant of most soil conditions and, being fully perennial, will remain healthy and vigorous for many years with the minimum of attention. They will grow equally well in shade or sun, though dappled sunlight suits them most of all, or a position where they are shaded from the midday heat. They bloom over many weeks, beginning in February when the climate is mild, and are at their best during spring and the early weeks of summer.

Nowhere do such plants look better than when growing in small beds. The 'knot' gardens of Elizabethan times suited them admirably. These were small beds made into the shape of hearts or circles, or a small piece of ground divided into squares, each filled with a different plant. The beds were edged or surrounded by low-growing plants which remain green all year and are also of neat habit, being tolerant of clipping, and growing no more than 10in tall. A suitable plant for this purpose is the native marjoram, although this is not as accommo-dating in this respect as the sweet marjoram, *Origanum marjorana*, a plant of the East. Featherfew, which is evergreen, makes a bushy plant if the flowers are removed, and could be used to surround the beds. It is easily raised from seed.

Also suitable is thrift, *Armeria maritima*, a maritime plant often used for this purpose in Tudor gardens. It may also be used to make up the beds themselves on account of its long-flowering season, the tiny rounded heads of mauve-pink appearing on leafless 6in stems. It blooms from May until September in a tuft of dark green grass-like leaves. The plant was used to decorate the threepenny piece of Elizabeth II's reign as this has always been a symbol of thrift. In earlier times it was known as ladies' cushion.

Plant these 10in apart in a well-drained soil to be successful and propagate by dividing the roots in spring. Keep the plants tidy by regularly removing the dead flowers which turn brown and do not drop, thus detracting from the display.

11 Pasque-flower

One of the most beautiful of our wild flowers is surely the pasque-flower, *Anemone pulsatilla*, which is occasionally found in downland country in Northamptonshire, Lincolnshire and south-east Yorkshire, always growing in chalk or limestone soils. It has now been named *Pulsatilla vulgaris*, but since earliest times has been known as the pasque or Easter flower because it flowers at Eastertide, during April and May. In the accounts of Edward I there is an item for colouring eggs at Eastertime with the bright green dye obtained from this plant.

It is low-growing, reaching a height of 4–5in, with thrice pinnate leaves covered in silky hairs. These appear after the flowers which are the size of a 10p piece and of the richest claret-purple, shaded pink on the reverse side, with striking golden anthers.

The pasque-flower is seen to advantage in small beds, set out about 12in apart, with care taken to see that the crown is not buried below the surface. They require a soil containing some humus and a little decayed manure, but mostly one containing plenty of lime rubble. The plants resent being disturbed and a bed should be left down for many years. It will be a glorious sight both before and after flowering, as the silky plumes of the seed heads persist through summer whilst the leaves are of richest grey-green, being almost fern-like. Top dress the soil occasionally with lime rubble and no other attention will be necessary.

There are several rare but equally beautiful varieties such as red clock with its velvety crimson flowers and, for contrast, the white-flowering *alba*.

Plants for Summer Display

The daisy in its double form, *Bellis perennis,* is a delightful plant for small beds coming into bloom in March, when only the primroses will be in colour. This makes an attractive edging for a bed of prim-roses, or for other low-growing plants, if the daisy plants are set out 4in apart. The bright green foliage is evergreen and in a mild winter there will be at least a few flowers in colour throughout the darkest days, the display continuing through spring and summer. The flower, a symbol of humility, figures in the insignia of Lady Margaret Beau-fort, mother of Henry VII by her marriage to Edmund Tudor.

Double daisies require a soil containing some humus for them to be long living, but they are readily raised from seed sown in April, or by division, which is necessary to perpetuate the named varieties. Of these, Dresden china, with its quilled petals of dusky pink, is one of the most delightful of all garden plants. It grows only 3in tall and is always in bloom. Rob Roy is a crimson companion for it. Similar in habit and in the quality of its bloom is the pomponette strain, bearing flowers in shades of pink, scarlet and crimson. Sutton's miniature strain is even shorter, growing only 2–3in tall, the colour range in-cluding shell pink, salmon and red.

A flower which it is always pleasant to come across in the wild is the marguerite, so called because it was taken as her emblem by Henry VI's queen, Margaret of Anjou, perhaps as a reminder of the alpine meadows of Anjou where the moon daisy flourishes. It has many other country names such as moon penny and ox-eye daisy, but its botanical name is *Chrysanthemum leucanthemum,* and it is indeed like a small single white chrysanthemum, growing about 15in tall with beautifully cut foliage of greyish-green. It was planted in large numbers by the Victorians as bedding to provide contrast to the Paul

12 Periwinkle

Crampel geranium. The plants were propagated from cuttings in a greenhouse or frame (as were geraniums) and grown on in small pots for bedding out in early June. It may also be raised from seed sown in gentle heat early in the year. Treat it in the same way as featherfew with which it may be used in small beds, and which is given the same cultural treatment.

The lesser periwinkle, *Vinca minor*, to be found in open woodlands and beneath hedgerows throughout Britain, is a most useful plant for small beds or for planting at the foot of a wall along which it will run. With its glossy dark evergreen leaves it always remains colourful, whilst its pale blue flowers continue almost uninterrupted throughout the year. As it grows well in shade it may also be used as ground cover for a shady bank. Chaucer called it 'the fresh pervinke, rich of hewe'. The plant takes its name from the Latin *vinco*, 'I conquer', for it will overcome all other plants growing near it. The double-flowered variety, *azurea flore plena*, has an intensity of colour equalled only by the gentian, whilst there is also a plum-coloured form, also double, called multiplex. The trailing stems of the periwinkle root easily, and, to propagate, all that is necessary is to detach a piece from the parent plant and reset it.

London pride, *Saxifraga umbrosa*, is a pretty plant for a shady bed or to edge a border of wild flowers. It is present on the craggy hills of Donegal and Mayo, also in one or two ravines in north Yorkshire where, originally obtained from the wild, it is to be found in every cottage garden. It possesses extreme hardiness and is evergreen, forming a rosette of glossy dark green leaves above which it bears sprays of pale pink flowers on 12in stems. The tiny petals are pointed with a delicacy seen in few other flowers and which may be fully appreciated only through a microscope. By Parkinson's time it had come to be planted in most London gardens, hence its familiar name, although Miss Alicia Coates, in *Flowers and Their Histories*, believes the plant received its name from George London, Royal Gardener to William III, who often used it for bedding and edging, and that it should really be known as London's pride. Readily propagated from seed, or by division in autumn, these should be planted 10in apart, and like some lime rubble in their diet.

The Primrose Family
The primrose, cowslip and oxlip, all of one family, are at their best in small beds shaded from the midday sun. They require a soil containing plenty of humus and, as they form their new roots around the crown of the plant almost at soil level, they will, more than any other plant, benefit from a yearly mulch of peat or leaf mould mixed with a little decayed manure. This should be given after flowering, working it up to the crown of the plant.

The primrose, *Primula vulgaris*, takes its name from *prima vera*, the first flower of springtime. By Shakespeare's time it had come to be called prime-rose and was a plant held in so great esteem that the word was used to denote excellence in all things. 'She is the pride and primrose of the rest', wrote Spenser.

The crinkled leaves enable every drop of dew and rain that falls on to them to be carried down to the roots in the shortest possible way and so quickly that little moisture can evaporate. The plants thrive on moisture and will soon perish in a dry soil, while in a soil well supplied with humus to retain the maximum amount of moisture they are almost indestructible. Though they will die back completely in winter, they begin to make new growth again early in spring when the first flower buds appear. The flowers have the ethereal beauty of palest moonlight—a paleness which poets often associated with death.

The primrose has always produced a great number of derivatives and doubles were widely planted in Tudor times—the double white known to Gerard may be obtained to this day, whereas the double yellow, described by Tabernaemontanus in 1500, is now rare. The

French variety, Marie Crousse, which has been more than a century in cultivation, still grows in many an old garden, beautifying the spring with its large double blooms of rich Parma violet, sometimes splashed with white, which have a delectable perfume.

Then there is the hose-in-hose form, where one flower grows out of another, Gerard called them 'two-in-hose' as two pairs of thick woollen stockings were always worn at one time, one stocking being pulled up to the thighs with another turned down below the knee, giving the appearance of one growing out of another, exactly like these flowers which have a dainty, feathery appearance. They were also known as duplex, or cup-and-saucer primroses. It is the primrose of Mrs Ewing's *Mary's Meadow*, the botanical explanation being that the lower bloom, of exactly similar colouring to the upper, is really a petaloid calyx. Derivatives in various shades of yellow are occasionally found in woodlands.

Another delightful form is the Jack-in-the-green or Jack-in-the-pulpit, where the flower is backed by a ruff composed of tiny replicas of the primrose leaf and of the same brilliant green. This is in marked contrast to the yellow or white of the flowers. The green ruff persists long after the flowers have died, and so the stems may be cut and used with other spring flowers in posy bowls even when the primroses have finished flowering.

Each of these forms may occasionally be found in the wild, but they are also obtainable from a few specialist growers who have stocks of many of these fascinating primroses. However, many have now become exceedingly rare and are collector's plants, priced accordingly, and these are described in detail in the author's book, *Growing Old Fashioned Flowers*, by the same publisher.

Primroses are readily raised from seed sown in spring in a frame, or in boxes containing John Innes compost and covered with a sheet of glass. Sow thinly and keep them comfortably moist. When large enough to handle, transplant the seedlings 1in apart to boxes or to open ground beds where they may grow on until November or early the following spring, when the plants can be moved to permanent beds. After two years they will be ready to divide, and this is done after flowering. After lifting, shake off all surplus soil and, holding the plant with both hands, gently 'tease' the pieces apart. They will come away readily with roots attached. Replant 6–8in apart.

Cowslips, *Primula veris*, are propagated in the same way and grow readily from seed. They require a more open situation and are usually found on downlands, growing in short grass, mostly on the side facing north or east, although they do enjoy some sunlight, while the primrose will grow in almost total shade. Britain has no more beautiful plant than the cowslip with its neat grey-green leaves and orange-yellow flowers, borne in clusters at the ends of 6in stems from April until June. Its calyx is the most delicate of all shades of green, and at the base of each flower is a small red spot. Shakespeare referred to this in *Cymbeline*, when Iachimo describes Imogen as having:

> On her left breast
> A mole, cinque-spotted, like the crimson drops
> I' the bottom of a cowslip.

The flowers have a refreshing perfume and take their name from the Saxon *cuslippe*, 'the breath of a cow'. Every part of the plant has its uses. The leaves (but do not remove too many) make a welcome addition to an early summer salad and a delicious wine is made from the flowers. A century ago, country children, who knew the flowers as 'paigles', made 'cucka-balls' of cowslip flowers, which were threaded on twine and suspended from one window to another across the street, as the Northamptonshire poet, John Clare so often mentioned:

> For they want some for tea and some for wine
> And some to maken up a cuckaball,
> To throw across the garland's silken line
> That reaches o'er the street from wall to wall.

There are two forms of the oxlip which is now a rare plant of the countryside. *Primula elatior*, the true oxlip, blooms in April and May. Its flowers resemble those of the cowslip, but are larger and are borne erect in a one-sided umbel. Buff-yellow in colour, they have the scent of ripe apricots. The oxlip is readily distinguished from the cowslip as its corolla-tube is without the five bosses. It is known as the Bardfield oxlip for it is now found only near the village of that name, in Essex.

The false oxlip is a natural hybrid evolved from the crossing of *P veris* (the cowslip) with *P vulgaris* (the primrose). It differs from *P elatior* in that its umbel is not one-sided, and the first flowers appear singly, like those of the primrose, only those appearing later resembling the cowslip. It enjoys a more open situation than the true oxlip and blooms at the same time. The flowers are a more golden yellow than those of *P elatior* and the funnel-like corolla has five bosses, absent in the true oxlip.

The false oxlip is the parent of the polyanthus, crossed with the Turkie-purple primrose introduced from the Caucasus by John Tradescant in the seventeenth century. This produced the red oxlip or polyanthus, first described by John Rea in his *Flora, Ceres and Pomona* in 1665. Twenty years later, Evelyn published his *Directions for the Gardener at Sayes Court* in which, for the first time, he mentioned the use of the red polyanthus for spring bedding. The now so common yellow polyanthus did not appear until 1880 when Miss Gertrude Jekyll discovered a plant growing wild in the garden at her home, Munstead, in Surrey, and from this plant she developed the famous Munstead strain.

The Violet and Pansy

Long before the birth of Christ, the violet, *Viola odorata*, was in commercial cultivation in Greece, as its sweetening properties were then much appreciated, and the flower became the symbol of ancient Athens. Later, the plants were grown in every cottage garden, for the flowers were cooked with meats and game and were candied to decorate cakes, just as they still are. In his *500 Points of Good Husbandry*, Thomas Tusser mentioned the violet as being suitable to grow in pots in sunny windows, so that the perfume could then be enjoyed indoors. Shakespeare knew about the quickly fading perfume of the flowers, referring to it in *Hamlet* when Laertes tells his sister, Ophelia, that Hamlet's affections are only:

> A violet in the youth of primy nature
> Forward, not permanent, sweet, not lasting,
> The perfume and suppliance of a minute;
> No more.

That the perfume so soon fades is due to the substance known as ionine, present in the chemical composition of the flower, and able to lessen the sense of smell in a very short time, so that it is not the flower which loses its fragrance but our own powers of smell which are dulled. If, after a few moments, the flower is inhaled again, its perfume can be enjoyed in all its strength.

Queen Victoria set a new fashion for violets, using the flowers in posies, not only for evening wear but in the daytime too. It was said that more than 4,000 violet plants were grown under frames at Windsor, to provide the Queen and the ladies of Court with a regular supply, and that double violets were the most popular, for they were the most heavily scented of all.

The violet is a perennial, reproducing long runners, like strawberries. It is happiest in the partial shade provided by other plants growing near it and a humus-laden soil containing a little decayed manure is necessary. Plant in autumn, 9in apart and propagate by detaching the runners at this time and replanting into beds of prepared soil. Double violets can only be grown south of the Thames.

Although it has no perfume, the common dog violet, *V canina*, which frequents mossy woodlands, is not to be despised for garden planting. It has heart-shaped leaves with flowers more blue than purple, and is distinguishable from *V odorata* by the pointed petals and more pronounced spur while it also blooms earlier. Enjoying partial shade, it is at its best in the garden in a shady bed and in a humus-laden soil. If kept moist during summer, it will usually bloom again in autumn.

The pansy or heartsease, *V tricolor*, has for centuries been everybody's favourite as a bedding plant, but it is an annual and it was not until the introduction of *V cornuta*, the alpine violet of the Pyrenees, exactly two centuries ago, and its use in breeding with our native species, that the pansy and viola took on a more perennial and tufted habit, better qualities for the flower garden.

The plant takes its name from the French *pensées*, 'thoughts'. 'And there is pansies—that's for thoughts', says Ophelia in *Hamlet*, in what must be one of the most touching of all Shakespeare's passages. Its country name of love-in-idleness which is used to this day in the Midlands would have been that most familiar to Shakespeare and he uses it in *A Midsummer Night's Dream* when Oberon bids Puck to obtain 'a little western flower called love-in-Idleness'. In Elizabeth

13 Wild pansy

Barber's *Glossary of Northamptonshire* (1854) appears the entry, 'Love in idleness—the small old-fashioned purple pansy also called Pinkeney John', yet another delightful name by which it was known and which shows the affection in which it was held. It was also called flamy because the colours of the flowers resemble those of the flames of burning wood. From the three colours of the flowers, the plant received its botanical name.

Gerard gives a description of it in his *Herbal* and also mentions the perennial or mountain pansy, *V lutea*, to be found in short downland turf, especially in northern England and in Scotland. He describes it accurately as 'a wild kinde having flowers of a feint yellow colour without mixture of any other colour, yet with a deeper yellow spot on the lower leaf [petal], with 4 or 5 blackish-purple lines. This is taken by some herbalists to be the yellow violet.' Parkinson calls it the 'Great Yellow Pansy . . . which better abideth our winters', meaning that it is of perennial habit, a quality it has passed on to the bedding viola. It was used by the Scottish nurseryman, James Grieve, known as the 'father of the bedding viola', in his breeding programme, together with *V amoena* which he collected at Moffat. The result was the first bedding violas which so quickly became popular with Victorian gardeners.

5

WILD FLOWERS FOR WALL AND PAVING

Flower of the solitary place!
Grey ruin's golden crown!
That lendest melancholy grace
To haunts of old renown.

David Macbeth Moir, *The Wallflower*

A number of our loveliest wild flowers are seen to advantage when growing in old walls or between paving stones. These may be planted on top of a wall made with a core of soil and built to divide one part of the garden from another. Here the plants will trail down the sides and, by their informal habit, will soften any hard appearance in a wall which has been newly built of stone or brick, bringing colour to the garden where it is most lacking. Many wild flowers are to be found growing in the cracks and crevices of mountainsides, often in the rocks themselves where there is perhaps sufficient weathered limestone and soil to support plantlife, the roots penetrating deep down in the search for whatever moisture they can find. The same conditions may be provided by an old wall, possibly built with a small quantity of mortar which has become broken down to a powder through the passing of time, and the same plants will also flourish here, their planting presenting no difficulty. A small amount of the mortar can be removed with a blunt knife and in its place a little fine soil pressed in. When planting pot-grown plants with the soil ball intact, press this directly into the opening and nothing more need be done. This is the best way to grow alpine plants whose roots will soon spread out between and beneath the moist stones. Several of our native pinks (or those long naturalised here) and also the stonecrops will grow well between the stones of an old wall. The wallflower, valerian and wall germander can also be grown in such places. Indeed, these plants will be happier between stones rather than in

garden soil for they resent an excess of moisture about their roots in
winter. In a wall, the winter rains will quickly drain away.

Plants in walls may also be grown from seed simply by mixing
some soil with the mortar and pressing in a seed or two. The seeds
will germinate more quickly, or plants will become established the
sooner, if the wall is given an occasional spraying in dry weather—
although not directly onto where the seed is sown for this may wash
out the compost. During periods of prolonged warm weather and
little rain, established wall plants will appreciate an occasional
syringing.

A number of the more compact plants, those of low, spreading
habit, may be planted between stone roofing tiles which are especially
attractive when covered in moss or lichens. *Sedum acre*, the stonecrop,
with its brilliant yellow flowers, is admirable when growing about
moss-covered tiles. Plants may also be grown from seed by pressing
a little soil between the tiles after dropping in a few seeds.

Making a Wall

Where making an old dry wall, stone, or cement blocks with a 'stone
finish', may be used. These are readily made with the Dry Pack
Concrete block-maker as manufactured by Higgs Foulkes of East
Ham. This simple tool enables blocks to be made at a rate of thirty per
hour for a cost of only 2p each. The mixture is three parts sand to one
part special stone-coloured cement, adding just sufficient water so
that the mixture will bind when squeezed, but no moisture will
exude.

A wall of 4–5ft will usually be high enough. A double wall will not
only prove more durable but will enable the centre cavity to be filled
with rubble to strengthen it, whilst topping this with 10in of soil will
enable a wide selection of wall plants to be grown. Where possible,
use a John Innes sterilised compost instead of garden soil so that weed
seeds will not be introduced.

Before building the wall, remove any soil or rubble to a depth of
10in and to the required length and width of the wall so that a 6in
concrete base may be provided. This should not be done during a
frosty period as it will cause the concrete to break up. Use a builder's
spirit level to ensure that the base is level.

Where building a wall with a central core, it is usual to make the wall about 18in wide, with a core 5–6in wide. Rubble is used at the base, and this must be pressed well down as the work proceeds, to give the wall exceptional strength. A stone wall will be stronger if a row of thicker stone alternates with one of smaller size stones but each individual row should be built with stones of similar size. If using bricks or uncut stone (and the same may be said of cement blocks) make sure that, where beginning another course, the stones are so placed that they will be directly above the joints of the previous row. This will add to the appearance and will greatly strengthen the wall. The core is topped with 12in of soil.

Another pleasing way of using stone in the garden is to build up a low wall, like a miniature rockery, alongside a path. It need be only 18in high and should be similar in width. Tufa stone (Westmorland limestone) is most suitable for this purpose. Alternatively, a retaining wall, in the shape of a rockery, can be made on either side of a flight of steps leading to a dell garden, where many bulbous wild flowers and others preferring partial shade may be grown. Small bulbs may also be planted about the steps and retaining wall.

The stone is obtainable from most alpine garden contractors and is the best stone to use for natural effect, for its layers can be seen clearly and it may be used to give the appearance of a natural outcrop, whilst it has many cracks and crevices in which small alpines may be planted. The porous nature of the stone enables the plants' roots to penetrate to considerable depths in their search for moisture and, against the grey stone, most of our alpine plants look entirely at home.

Plants for Walls

One of the most loved of our wild flowers is the wallflower, *Cheiranthus cheiri*, a perennial with an erect woody stem which is much branched. When in bloom in April, May and June it makes a veritable mound of colour, the flowers being orange-yellow with a pronounced violet perfume. The scent is highly complex and the main elements of the violet, rose, hawthorn and orange blossom have been isolated from its attar.

To the early English it was known as chevisaunce, 'the comforter', because of its warm, comforting perfume. The poet Milton coupled it with the pansy in his *Lycidas*:

The pretty paunce and the chevisaunce
Shall match with the faire flower-de-luce.

Parkinson wrote that 'the sweetness of the flowers causes them to be
used in nosegays', hence its botanical name, *Cheiranthus*, 'hand-
flower', for the blossoms were carried by ladies on special occasions.
It is found growing on old castle walls everywhere, but is nowhere
more prevalent than on those of the Lowlands of Scotland. Sir
Walter Scott leaves us in no doubt as to his affection for it in his
lines:

The rude stone-face, with wallflowers gay,
To me more pleasure yield
Than all the pomp imperial domes display.

Wallflowers are easily raised from seed sown in drills in June, and
the plants moved to pockets of soil in walls or to the border in the
early autumn. They will bloom the following spring and, if left
alone, will do so for many years, though in the garden they are
usually pulled up after flowering as they are so easily raised from
seed each year. There is a lovely double form named after the Rev
Harpur Crewe who discovered it, which is propagated only from
cuttings.

The snapdragon, *Antirrhinum majus*, is also perennial. A native of
Central Europe, it reached Britain possibly with the Romans or with
the Norman invaders. It is found on old walls, as at St Augustine's
Abbey, Canterbury, and was firmly established as a garden plant by
Tudor times, being included by Lyte in his *New Herbal*, described as
'not much unlike the flowers of toadflax'. Henry Phillips tells of
finding it 'on the cliffs of Dover', saying that 'on pressing the sides of
the flower, it opens like a gaping mouth', hence its country name of
snapdragon.

Plants are usually raised in heat early in the year and, after harden-
ing, are set out towards the end of May, coming into bloom in July
and continuing until the end of autumn.

The common valerian, *Valeriana officinalis*, which grows 2ft tall, is
frequently found about limestone cliffs and growing from the top of
old castle walls. Its pale pink flowers, borne in a terminal cyme, have
a tube 5mm long, and depend upon butterflies for their pollination.

A handsome plant with dark green pinnate leaves, it takes its name from the Latin, *valere* 'to be well', hence its country name of all-heal. A decoction of the roots was taken for nervous exhaustion whilst cats will become almost intoxicated if they should nibble at them. Plants are readily raised from seed sown in the open ground in April and will come into bloom the following year.

One of the loveliest of wall plants is the Fountains Abbey pink, a form of either *Dianthus caryophyllus* or *D plumarius*, the common pink, with its toothed petals and flesh-pink flowers, measuring about 1½in across. The plant is native to Europe, but must have reached England with the Normans. Today, *D plumarius* is found on the walls of Fountains Abbey, Yorkshire, and at Rochester Castle, Kent, with its roots in the mortar, lime being the most important part of the diet of all *Dianthus*. They bloom in July, and it is believed that their old name of 'gillyflower' was a corruption of 'July-flower', although to the old writers every clove-scented flower was known as a 'gilly-flower'. Thus we have stock gillyflower and wall gillyflower, the latter being better known to us as the wallflower. In the 'Prologue' to the *Canterbury Tales*, Chaucer tells of:

> . . . many a clove giolfre,
> And notemuge to put in ale,
> Whether it be moist or stale . . .

As the pilgrims set out from the Tabard Inn at Southwark, they would have drunk wine or ale flavoured with the clove-scented pinks, which grew in all alehouse gardens and flowered in midsummer. They were known as 'sops in wine'. When the plant was not in bloom, nutmeg was used to impart a similar flavour to ale, which was then made without hops.

The pink gave its name to our language, a word denoting the flesh colour of its flowers, though it was not until late in the eighteenth century that the word 'pink' came into general use. The plant was possibly called pink from the Celtic *pic* meaning 'peak'—perhaps in this case 'peak of perfection'.

The Cheddar pink, *D caesius*, native to southern Europe and found in Britain only in the most inaccessible parts of the Cheddar Gorge, is now a protected plant. One of the loveliest of all our wild flora, it forms a spreading mat (hence its name of matted pink) of short greyish-blue leaves and bears its clove-scented fringed flowers of deep pink during June and July. Writing of this plant in 1949, the late Will Ingwersen said: 'It possesses all the virtues one sees in a rock plant . . . It is easily pleased, asking only a sunny aspect and a well-drained soil. It is an exceedingly attractive wall plant and may also be used in the crevices between paving stones.' Most specialist growers have these plants for sale, or they may be readily grown from seed.

D deltoides, the maiden pink, is equally effective. It is also a native plant and is almost as rare, occasionally being found on grassy, mountainous slopes. It will form a prostrate mat growing between stones, or will cascade from the top of an old wall, its deep green foliage being evergreen, whilst its dark pink flowers with their toothed petals remain colourful from June until August. The form known as brilliant has vivid crimson-red flowers and, for contrast, there is a white form, *alba*.

A most interesting plant is the navelwort, *Cotyledon umbilicus*, for long known to cottagers as the wall pennywort. It takes its botanical name from the Greek, *kotule*, 'a dish', from the saucer-shaped leaves. Gerard called it the great navelwort and described the flowers as being 'incarnate' coloured, or flesh, from which the word carnation was derived. Gerard tells us that the plant was to be found growing from the walls of Westminster Abbey 'over the door that leadeth from Chaucer's tomb to the old Palace'. This is what makes Gerard so interesting: always he tells us exactly where he saw the plants growing in their natural state.

The cup-shaped leaves are held on stalks 2in long whilst the succulent flower stems will attain a height of 12in, the greenish-white flowers, like tiny bells, being held in racemes. They bloom from early June until the end of August when the entire plant takes on an attractive pinkish tint. It is a member of the stonecrop family, like the wall pepper, *Sedum acre*, which has similar fleshy leaves, enabling it to store up moisture to carry it through a period of dry weather. *S acre* forms a spreading mat and, during June and July, covers itself in a sheet of brilliant yellow star-like flowers.

S rupestre, the rock stonecrop, is occasionally present about rocky places in walls, its yellow flowers arising from a rosette of fleshy leaves. The white stonecrop, *S album*, is present on dry walls every-

Plate 7 Single scented peony, *Paeonia coralina*

Plate 8 The primrose, *Primula vulgaris*

Plate 9 Common star of Bethlehem, *Ornithogalum umbellatum*

where, its white flower-heads held above fleshy dark green leaves. The English stonecrop, *S anglicum*, is equally prevalent. It forms clusters of white star-like flowers on stems 2–3in tall and, like *S album*, blooms from June until August. The rose-root, *S rosea*, may also be seen on old walls but will grow equally well in a border, where its grey over-lapping leaves, continuing all the way up the 8in stem, and heads of greenish-yellow flowers in May and June, make it a most handsome plant for the front of a border. A pleasant rose water can be made from the dried roots.

Of the closely related saxifrages, *Saxifraga hypnoides*, the mossy saxifrage, to be found on rocky outcrops from Cheddar to North Wales, flowers in May and June, its pinkish-white flowers appearing on 3in stems above a prostrate mat of mossy foliage. There is a form, known as *densa*, in which the foliage turns crimson in autumn. The yellow mountain saxifrage, *S aizoides*, is equally attractive with thick narrow fleshy leaves, and bearing bright yellow flowers from June until August. A natural hybrid, *S burnattii* bears pure white flowers on crimson stems.

The golden saxifrage, which is not really a saxifrage at all but *Chrysosplenium oppositifolium*, is occasionally found on rocks, although it prefers wet, shady places where it forms mats of round, long-stalked pale green leaves and bears tiny yellow flowers in March.

Teucrium chamaedrys, the wall germander, is occasionally found on old monastic walls in the south. It is a striking plant, with dark green oval leaves and, in July and August, spikes of crimson-purple flowers on 8in stems. Possibly introduced by the Normans, it was widely used for strewing, being included amongst Tusser's list of herbs for this purpose. Parkinson, writing of those plants suitable for 'knotted' beds or for edging a small border, said of germander (and hyssop): 'they must be kept in some form and proportion by cutting, and the cuttings are much used as strewing herbs for houses, being pretty and sweet, with a refreshing lemony scent'. Dr Leminius, a Dutch physician on a visit to England in 1560, writing of the Englishman's home, said: 'their chambers and parlours strewed with fresh herbs refreshed me, their nosegays finely intermingled with sundry sorts of fragrant flowers, in their bed chambers and privi rooms with comfortable smell, cheered me up and entirely delighted my senses'. The leaves may be dried and used in pot pourris to which they impart

D

a smell like that of balm. In this way, Culpeper said, 'It is good against a continual headache, melancholy, drowsiness, and dullness of the spirits.'

Another labiate, the mountain thyme, *Thymus serpyllum*, is also seen to advantage on walls and is especially useful to plant between paving stones, for it forms a prostrate spreading mat, its serpent-like stems being so tough that they do not mind being trodden upon. The flowers, with their red calyx and rose-coloured corolla are borne in terminal heads from June until August. The name is probably derived from the Greek *thumos*, 'smoke', a reference to the use of the dried stems in sacrifices because of their pleasant odour when burnt, and its later use in places of worship. The plant is anti-spasmodic, good for relief of nervous tension and headaches, whilst 'boiled in wine and drunk, it is good against the warblings and rumblings of the belly'. A few drops of oil of thyme placed in a jug of hot water and inhaled, will relieve a stuffy feeling caused by a head cold.

There are several colourful varieties, pink chintz bearing a flower of richer pink than the common type, whilst *coccineus* bears mats of brilliant crimson.

T drucei is equally suitable for walls and paving, the elliptic leaves being covered in minute glandular dots which, when trodden upon, release a pleasant aromatic perfume. Above them, the reddish-purple flowers, so often visited by bees, are borne in whorls and are colourful from May until the end of summer. The plant is present on dry banks and old walls, on heaths and downlands throughout the British Isles. Shakespeare knew well the bank where the 'wild thyme grows', and Shelley wrote of 'the bees on the bells of thyme'.

The prostrate thymes may be planted 12in apart with *Sedum acre*, to make a colourful 'lawn' or plot, possibly alongside a path—a thyme alley—as Francis Bacon suggested. In twelve months, they will have completely covered the soil and will 'buzz' with honey bees all summer. It was because of the activity of bees as they worked the flowers that the plant became the symbol of action and valour in the days of chivalry. Ingram, in his *Flora Symbolica*, wrote that ladies 'embroidered their knightly lover's scarves with the figure of a bee hovering about a sprig of thyme'. 'To smell of thyme' came to be an expression of praise.

The common calamint, *Calamintha ascendens*, another labiate, is also perfectly at home on an old wall or growing between paving stones. It has oval dark green leaves and from July until September bears a one-sided spike of dainty mauve-pink flowers of 12in stems. The foliage is pleasantly scented.

The closely related self-heal, *Prunella vulgaris*, a creeping downy perennial, which bears its purple flowerheads on 6in stems throughout summer, grows well on a wall. A decoction of the leaves was once used to treat wounds, or the leaves bound around cut skin to bring about rapid healing.

The knotted pearlwort, *Sagina nodosa*, found in barren places, usually near the sea, is a pretty perennial for a wall. It grows 4–6in tall, with short leaves borne in clusters, like knots, along the thin, wiry stems, whilst in August and September it bears white flowers which are quite large for so small a plant.

S procumbens, the mossy pearlwort, is another species which grows well between stones, forming a clump of bright green moss above which it bears tiny greenish flowers all summer. It has its uses, but tends to spread between the stones rather too vigorously, and often takes over, to the exclusion of other plants.

There are several members of the cabbage or *Cruciferae* family which do well on old walls. An interesting plant is the wall rocket, *Diplotaxis tenuifolia*. It is perennial, growing 18–20in tall. The leaves are divided into narrow segments and are most handsome, though they release a fetid smell when handled. The small pale yellow flowers, however, are pleasantly scented and are worked by bees. It is more common in southern England, as is sweet alyssum, *Alyssum maritimum*, possibly a garden escapee, but often seen on old walls, the entire plant having the refreshing smell of newly mown hay. This makes a neat spreading mound with linear leaves and bears clusters of small white flowers from June until late September. It is used in gardens for edging summer bedding plants.

The Garden Path

There are a number of wild flowers which are admirable for planting about paving stone used to make a terrace or garden path. Small bulbs and other plants, preferably those with a low, spreading habit, may be planted in the pockets between the stones.

When making a path of crazy paving, begin by marking out the necessary length and width. Then remove several inches of soil to the depth of the stone (for this purpose the mellow, honey-coloured York stone is best). A better job will be done if lengths of timber, 6in wide and ¾in thick, are placed along the sides where the path is to be made, the timber being held in place by stout stakes driven into the ground and cut level with the top edge of the timber. (Two rows of bricks placed on their side will answer the same purpose.) The path need not be in straight lines, and will in fact look better in gentle undulating curves which follow the contours of the border.

For the base, place a layer of shingle or sand to a depth of about 2in and make it quite firm. Position the stones so that there is as little space between them as possible and so that the straight edges are flush to the boards. If laying stones which have been cut square or into various rectangular shapes, this will present no problem in sorting out the stone, but be sure to plan the path to the correct width of the stones, so that it will not be necessary to cut them. A path should be not less than 18–20in wide, though 2ft is preferable.

The only tools required are a good spade and a builder's spirit level, so that the stones can be laid flat, although a stake placed across the path will ensure that the stones are level with (or just below) the top of the boards and the surrounding ground. If the path is made in a lawn this will enable the mower to be taken over the sides of the path (or one side of it) when the lawn is being cut.

Laying the stone is best done in sections of about 2yd, filling in the cracks between the stones with sand and leaving small pockets at intervals. These are filled with compost when the path is finished and seeds sown or plants set in them, while plants from small pots, with the soil ball intact, may be pressed in. Remember to place the stones so that the flat side is uppermost, otherwise they will prove difficult to walk upon.

Small bulbs can be planted with the alpine plants so that they will grow up through them and will give colour at a time when the alpine plants may not be in bloom.

The Trough Garden

A number of these plants may also be used in a trough garden. *Sedum acre* and the creeping thymes, the saxifrages and cushion pinks, also the double daisy, are all suitable and enjoy the same soil conditions— a well-drained soil containing some sand and lime rubble, obtainable from old buildings. In addition, several of the miniature native bulbs can be planted, such as *Scilla verna*, the snowdrop, winter aconite, the crocus and wild daffodil. They will bring colour to the trough garden during winter and spring, before the other plants come into bloom.

The stone trough has, for centuries, been a feature of the cottage garden, for weathered stone will blend perfectly with the stone of the cottage and outbuildings, or with an old stone wall in which many of the same plants will be growing. Or a trough may be made of concrete, which will be porous and so ensure efficient drainage whilst keeping the soil sweet. The trough may be placed on a balcony, on the sunny side of a courtyard, or beneath the eaves of a house, and will be most appreciated beneath a window where the plants may be enjoyed from indoors. However, it is important that the trough is not placed beneath mature trees from which rain will drip, causing the soil to become consolidated, while fallen leaves give it an untidy appearance.

To make a concrete trough, construct two boxes of timber, making one 1½in smaller in all dimensions so as to fit inside the larger box. For the base and walls of the trough, mix two parts of sand to one part cement, adding sufficient water to make it into a paste that will pour freely, but not be too sloppy. To reinforce the base and sides, strips of small-mesh wire netting are placed across the bottom of the larger box and up the two opposite sides. For drainage holes, two large, thick corks are placed at the bottom of the larger box, one at each end. Cut the netting to the exact measurements of the larger box. Thus, for a box 30in × 18in × 6in deep, the two pieces of netting will measure 42in and 30in long. The smaller box does not require a base. Simply make the sides and, when placed inside the other, hold in position, 1½in above the base of the larger box, by nailing four thin pieces of timber across the corners. The cement mixture is then poured down the sides and left for twenty-four hours to set hard. Then carefully remove the inner box, but do not press out the corks before removing the outer box and rendering the sides of the trough with a mixture of cement and crushed stone to hide the wire netting and give the trough a natural appearance. When quite dry (its making should be done in an open shed, or in a cellar or outhouse, to ensure that it remains dry until it has set hard) two people will be needed to move the trough to a suitable position where it should be placed on stones at the required height.

The trough should then be filled with a strong solution of permanganate of potash to neutralise the concrete. Fill to the top and leave for several days, then removing the corks to catch the liquid in buckets. Rinse out with clean water and the trough is ready to fill with compost.

First place a large 'crock' over the drainage holes and, at the bottom, a 1in layer of shingle. Fill to within ½in of the top, using a compost made up of two parts turf loam and one part each sand and lime rubble. Mix well together and allow it two to three days to settle before putting in the plants and bulbs.

6

A WILD-FLOWER ROCK GARDEN

For a shelf among rocks, the milkworts,
the sky blue, the white, and the pink;
with these I float out May like Fra Angelico.

Maurice Hewlett, *Rest Harrow*

Most of those plants which grow in the most inaccessible places, high up on rock faces and ledges, particularly in Westmorland and Cheddar Gorge, as well as in the Burren of western Ireland, Snowdonia and parts of Scotland, are suitable for planting in an alpine garden. I am thinking particularly of those plants usually found growing high up on the walls of old abbeys and castles, as described in Chapter 5. However, there are other plants of equal beauty, such as the birdseye primula, *Primula farinosa*, and the spring-flowering gentian, glorious with its brilliant blue trumpets against the weathered grey limestone of northern England.

Making a Rock Garden

An alpine garden should appear when it is finished as though it was part of the mountainous landscape, with the plants arranged as they would be in their natural haunts. Made on the flat, as it often will be, it should be so constructed as to represent a level outcrop where the stone has weathered into gentle undulations and rock fragments have gathered about them. Here, humus will begin to form and soon the plants will be able to flourish between the harder rocks that have resisted wind and weather. Limestone and sandstone should be laid down in layers all sloping in the same direction, the stones following a gentle incline. Westmorland limestone is the best of all rockery stone for it will have formed pockets and crevices into which the plants may be set, whilst it also has a beautifully weathered appearance. It is frost-resistant as well and its grey colour contrasts with the small and brilliantly coloured corollas of many of our dwarf plants and bulbs. Sandstone is also effective but is more difficult to arrange and for a time will look red and raw, while frost will cause it to flake.

When making a small alpine garden it is better to use pieces of stone of average size throughout, although always avoiding the use of too many small pieces which give the rockery a 'bitty' appearance, for it is never easy to arrange them in a natural-looking outcrop. When ordering stone from a specialist supplier, impress upon him that too many small stones are not required. Once the stone is on site, the work should proceed slowly, and with care.

First dig out the soil to the area the rockery (alpine garden) is to occupy, to a depth of about 6in, throwing up the soil a little towards the back to give the rockery a gentle slope, facing the house if possible. When the base has been excavated, place in it a 3in layer of clinker, boiler ash, crushed brick, or small stone to provide efficient drainage.

For a level site the stone should consist of long flat pieces—a bank requiring stone with high 'faces', a flat rockery requiring stone with less 'face' but more 'top'. The 'face' shows the layers, the softer parts having been eroded by the wind and rain driving against it. The 'top' is where the rain beats down on it and where standing water will have worn it into rounded holes and crevices in which the plants are set.

In constructing the rockery, the 'face' of the stone should always look to the front with the 'top' upwards. A flat site may be built downwards, upwards or sideways, bedding the rocks into the drainage material and making each higher at the 'face' than at the back so that it slants away from the angle of the slope. If sloping to the front, rain will wash away the soil from the cracks and hollows. However, only a slight difference in height is necessary, the backwards slope being very gentle, with every stone treated in the same way.

Instead of dotting the stones about here and there, concentrate them so that they fit together, one behind the other, like the sides of a ravine. Place a few stones across the mouth of the ravine, with a flat planting space behind them, to imitate a stream or waterfall. Use long stones, pointing the way the 'stream' would flow, but always facing forward with the top upwards. If the site is flat, the strata lines on the 'faces' should also be flat. Always think of the rockery as being one large natural rock with parts showing through the soil. To make a rockery on a low bank, insert the stone into the bank after removing the grass. Use the stones with the largest 'face' at the top, with the flat surface uppermost and sloping in the same direction, which should be gently backwards. If the bank is steep, it may be possible to make an extension at the bottom, thus lessening the acuteness of the angle.

Between the stones, the soil is added, ramming it down as the work proceeds. The soil should consist of loam and peat in equal parts by bulk, but, before mixing together, make the peat thoroughly moist. After mixing, the compost should bind together when squeezed, but no moisture should exude through the fingers.

Autumn is possibly the most suitable time to make up a rockery, for then the dwarf spring-flowering bulbs such as *Scilla verna* and winter aconite can be planted in groups of three or four, to bloom in spring.

Plants raised from seed should be grown on in small pots so that they may be planted out without disturbing their roots. They are planted in any holes and in the crevices between the stones where they will at once begin to send out their roots into the porous Westmorland rock and where, in summer, they will retain their freshness during long periods of dry weather. The plants should, however, be watered whenever necessary, and must also be kept free from weeds by looking over the rockery at regular intervals and removing any weeds before they become large. In autumn, remove any dead leaves which may have fallen on the rockery and give the plants a top dressing made up of a mixture of peat and fibrous loam. At this time also, remove any dead flowers and leave the rockery clean and tidy for the winter.

Suitable Alpine Plants

Those plants of semi-trailing habit, such as *Dianthus deltoides*, the maiden pink, and the soapwort, *Saponaria officinalis*, are admirable for the alpine garden, trailing over the stones, their deep pink flowers blending to perfection with the grey Westmorland limestone. What is more, these plants enjoy a measure of lime in their diet and will thrive under such conditions. Likewise the white and yellow stonecrops, *Sedum album* and *S acre*, are colourful in July and August with their masses of tiny flowers, while the plants form a mat of brilliant green which spreads over and around the stones until they are almost completely hidden from view. The large yellow stonecrop, *S reflexum*, which has greyish foliage and large yellow flowerheads is equally handsome. The wall pennywort, of the same family, should also be planted for it is as much at home in a rockery as on a wall.

The pink oxalis, *Oxalis floribunda*, so long in bloom, and the bloody cranesbill, *Geranium sanguineum*, its lurid crimson flowers strikingly lovely against grey limestone, are both plants to grace the rock garden; likewise the common rock-rose, *Helianthemum chamaecistus*, with its cups of brilliant gold and *H apenninum*, the white rock-rose with its downy grey foliage and pure white flowers, a plant which is common amongst the rocks around Torquay in Devon.

The rock-roses are plants of shrubby habit; so, too, is the rock-spray, *Cotoneaster microphyllus*, a prostrate evergreen which will soon cover a large stone with its stems of glossy leaves, its white flowers being followed by large crimson berries. It is frequently found growing on rocky hillsides of limestone formation and is a garden escapee, growing from seed dropped by birds, for the plant originally came from the Himalayas early in the nineteenth century. One form, *thymifolius*, is an even more suitable rock-garden plant with its narrow deep green leaves and compact habit.

A rare plant of limestone formations of northern England and of the Burren is the spring gentian, *Gentiana verna*, one of the most attractive of wild flowers, its upright trumpets of deepest blue appearing after the snows and continuing until mid-June. The flowers

14   Spring gentian

arise on stems 2in tall from a rosette of greyish leaves which act as a perfect foil. It is perennial and is one of the few gentians to flourish in an alkaline soil. The Easter flower, *Pulsatilla vulgaris*, would prove a suitable plant to accompany the gentian on the rockery for it blooms at the same time and is found under the same natural conditions.

Another plant of outstanding beauty is the birdseye primrose, *Primula farinosa*, to be found occasionally on limestone formations, usually sheltering from the winter rains beneath a hood of overhanging rock. And this is where it should be planted in the rock garden for its leaves, which are covered in farina (down), hold moisture and are liable to decay in prolonged wet weather. The plant forms a grey-green rosette and in May and June its flowers are borne in an umbel at the end of a leafless stalk 5–6in tall. The lilac-pink flowers have a conspicuous yellow eye, like that of a blackbird.

Other members of the primula family to enjoy rock garden conditions are the cowslip, primrose and the creeping jenny, *Lysimachia nummularia*, a perennial with almost round leaves and creeping stems. From the leaf joints it bears tiny bell-shaped flowers of golden yellow which open star-like. Rather similar in habit is the trailing St John's wort, *Hypericum humifusum*, its small elliptical leaves and tiny yellow flowers having numerous black dots which are resinous glands. It is in bloom from June until the end of summer.

The alpine pearlwort, *Sagina saginoides*, also has slim stems of trailing habit, each of which arises from a rosette of linear leaves. At the end of the stems, a tiny pearl-like flower appears. The knotted pearlwort, *S nodosa*, also perennial, is of more upright habit with 'knots' at the leaf joints all along the stems, at the end of which appears the tiny white flower.

The arabis, *Arabis caucasica*, a garden escapee, is an admirable rock-garden plant with long toothed leaves of greyish-green and bearing, in April and May, several slightly scented pure white flowers on 6in stems. It has become established on limestone formations around Grindleford in north Derbyshire, and elsewhere in that region. The alpine pennycress, *Thlaspi alpestre*, also perennial, is found in the same area. It too has grey-green leaves and white or lilac flowers, borne on 9in stems, from April until June.

The starry saxifrage, *Saxifraga stellaris*, is also perennial and is happiest growing between the cracks of Westmorland stone. From a rosette of greyish leaves arises a 6in stem, at the end of which appear numerous small white flowers which open like twinkling stars and remain in bloom from June until late in August.

The yellow mountain saxifrage, *S aizoides*, in bloom at the same time, forms a thick mat of lanceolate leaves from which arise red stems, at the end of which tiny yellow flowers with red anthers will appear. It is rather like the marsh saxifrage which prefers a moist soil although its yellow flowers are almost twice the size.

The mossy saxifrage, *S hypnoides* (syn: *S rosacea*), forms a moss-like mat above which it bears, in May and June, nodding flowers of pinkish white. The purple saxifrage, *S oppositifolia*, is also a plant for the rock garden. It is a trailing prostrate perennial with small oval leaves, being almost thyme-like in appearance, with a quite large flower of deepest purple at the end of each stem. It is found on limestone outcrops from north Yorkshire to the Scottish Highlands and also in the north-west of Ireland, flowering during April and May.

The closely related common sundew, *Drosera rotundifolia*, a perennial, is also at its best on the rockery, provided some peat is incorporated about its roots and it can be constantly provided with moisture, for it is at home in boggy ground on moorlands and requires an acid soil. It, too, forms a rosette of pale green leaves which are covered with crimson hairs. These are sticky and when a small fly crawls over the leaves, the hairs enclose it, preventing its escape so that it may be digested by the plant. The white flowers are borne in small umbels at the end of the leafless stem which arises 6in high from the centre of the rosette.

The rock sea lavender, *Limonium binervosum*, which produces its lavender flowers at the end of 6in stems in August and September, and the previously mentioned thrift, are both perennials, found about rocky formations close to the sea, which will grow equally well on a rockery.

Like the purple saxifrage, the moss campion, *Silene acaulis*, is found on mountainous slopes in northern England, including the Lake District, and also in Wales and Northern Ireland. A perennial, it is a dainty little plant growing 6in tall and forming a mat of tiny linear leaves above which it bears multitudes of rosy-red star-like flowers in June and July. With it may often be found the pretty alpine mouse-ear, *Cerastium alpinum*, of the same pink family of plants. A perennial, with oval leaves covered in short hairs like a mouse's ears, in June and July it bears a solitary large white flower at the end of a 4in stem.

The starwort mouse-ear, *C cerastoides*, is equally dainty and bears its white flowers during July and August, on 3in stems.

The dainty milkworts, prostrate perennials of downlands and bearing their tiny flowers of sky blue, pink and white, from early May until the end of summer, could also be included in the alpine garden. They are easily raised from seed.

The harebell, *Campanula rotundifolia*, is found everywhere on grassy slopes. It is equally lovely in the alpine garden for it is fully perennial.

The alpine forget-me-not, *Myosotis alpestris*, scented at night, is a plant worthy of inclusion in the rock garden. Mostly found in Scotland, it has small greyish leaves and bears its royal blue flowers in short erect spikes during July and August—being by far the latest of the forget-me-nots. It requires a well-drained soil to be long lasting.

Often present in the same mountainous regions of Scotland is the fascinating little alpine speedwell, *Veronica alpina*, a perennial with blue-green foliage, which bears its deep blue flowers in short erect terminal spikes at the very same time as the alpine forget-me-not. The plant is often confused with the mountain speedwell, *V tenella*, but this has creeping, rather than erect, stems and roots from the leaf joints.

Also Scottish in its habitat is the charmingly named St Olaf's candlestick, the one-flowered wintergreen, *Pyrola uniflora*, a perennial in every way as delightful as its name. It has pale green leaves and bears a deliciously scented waxy white bell-shaped flower at the end of a 6in stem. Flowering in June and July, it grows only in pine woods and needs an acid soil, so work in some peat or pine needles around its roots and it will be as long living as any plant.

The common wintergreen, *P minor*, a perennial growing 6in tall and bearing its pale pink bell-shaped flower during June and July, is widespread on moorlands and mountainous slopes in northern England and in Scotland, and also requires an acid soil. The flower spike is produced from a rosette of toothed leaves.

These plants are closely connected to the heath family of which the ling, *Calluna vulgaris* (and its varieties), is suitable for rock-garden planting. One of the best forms is Ruth Sparks which has strikingly beautiful golden foliage in winter and bears double flowers of purest white. It grows only 10in tall. Likewise Joan Sparks which bears double flower spikes of deepest pink in August and September. Orange queen with its gold and bronze foliage is also compact.

7

WILD FLOWERS FOR THE WATER GARDEN

And nearer to the river's trembling edge
There grew broad flag-flowers, purple
                    prank't with white,
And starry river buds amongst the sedge,
And floating water-lilies, broad and bright . . .

Shelley, *The Question*

A pond or pool in the garden, whether natural or manmade, stocked with ornamental fish and with suitable plants by the side, will be a place of interest throughout the year. Birds will visit it to drink and catch small flies which hover above the water, but mostly it will be a place where a whole range of wild flowers can be grown which would not flourish under ordinary garden conditions, for these plants must have moisture about their roots. Where there is a natural pool, or water running through the garden, the plants may be set out along its banks and little else need be done. A pool may also be made quite easily in a corner of the garden away from overhanging trees which will foul the water with their dead leaves.

Having selected a suitable position for a pool (the most economical use of the garden will be made where the pool is in one corner), mark out the position and shape with thick twine, then remove the turf or soil to a depth of at least 3in and 12in from the edge of the pool. This will be where many of the moisture-loving plants will be set out, together with those to be planted on the marginal shelf. Using the twine, which is held in place by stakes as a guide, remove the soil so that the pool sides have an inward slope of 3in for every 9in in depth. An average sized pool should be 2ft deep if of an area of up to 120sq ft, with a marginal shelf 9in wide and 6in below the edge of the pool. If a pool is made less than 50sq ft in area, it will be

difficult to keep it clear of algae and food contamination. It is necessary to strike a balance between fish and plantlife, and a pool correctly
made will keep itself clean and require emptying and cleaning only
once in every five years.

When the soil has been removed to the required depth, use a spirit
level to ensure that the base and shelf are level, otherwise the plants
at one end will receive too much water above their roots, whilst the
others will have too little. The shelf and the base of the pool must be
smooth and free of all stones so that the liner will not tear when the
pool is filled with water.

A Butylite liner is flexible and has a life of at least fifteen years. It
may be blue, reflecting the colour of the water, or stone-coloured.
When the area is ready, the liner is draped in, held in place at the
edge by large stones. As the pool is filled with water, ease off the
liner so that it fits into the base and marginal shelves, leaving a 3in
overlap around the edge. This is covered with a 3in depth of soil so
that, after removing 12in of turf around the side, there will be 9in of
soil in which moisture-loving plants are set.

The size of liner required for the pool is calculated by: the length
of the pool + twice the depth × the width + twice the depth. The
pool can be circular, kidney-shaped or rectangular, the width and
length calculated from the widest point.

The most suitable time to make a pool is in April and May when
the marginal plants begin to make new growth. Those plants with
their roots under water, eg the water-lilies and oxygenators, are
planted in containers, known as crates, which are made of polythene.
Their use eliminates the need for a layer of soil in the pool and so
ensures clearer water. The crates are lined with sacking and then
placed in the water, sometimes on a brick or breeze block, depending
upon the depth of water they require. The crates are filled with a
good loamy soil before the plants are set in them. A small crate will
hold one water-lily or six oxygenating plants which are pushed into
the soil and will root in a few days under water. Without these, the
water will turn thick and green because of the algae which appear
with the action of sunlight upon the mineral salts. The oxygenating
plants absorb both and so prevent the algae from forming to any
great degree.

Plate 10 Meadowsweet, *Spiraea ulmaria*

Plate 11 Nodding star of Bethlehem, *Ornithogalum nutans*

Plate 12 Wood tulip, *Tulipa sylvestris*

Planting the Pool

The most beautiful of all water plants are the water-lilies which require a depth of 6in of water to begin with, so their crates should stand on several blocks. As the leaves form, one or more of the blocks is removed until, after a year, the crate is resting on the bottom of the pool. Two species only are native plants, *Nymphaea alba*, which bears fragrant white flowers in July and August, about 6in across, with large golden stamens, and *Nuphar lutea*, with yellow flowers of about half the size and smelling of brandy, hence its name of brandy-bottle. The leaves and flowers float on the surface. *N lutea* blooms over a longer period, from June until September. There is a smaller variety (pigmy) of both species, which is suitable for very small pots or for planting in oak tubs. From *Nymphaea alba* several beautiful hybrid varieties have been raised, such as albatross which has snow-white flowers and pale green leaves and is suitable for a small pond.

Several of the deep marginal plants should be used as they will reduce the amount of sunlight reaching the water, as well as providing shade and shelter for fish. Like the lilies, they should be placed on blocks and lowered by degrees to the bottom of the pool as they become established.

Of the three chief deep-water plants, *Hottonia palustris*, *Aponogeton distachyum* and *Orontium aquaticum*, only the first is a native plant. It is perennial and produces whorls of pale green leaves which remain submerged while above the surface, often to a height of 12in or more, rise spikes of pale pink flowers with the scent of violets, hence its name of water violet. It blooms during May and June.

A delightful little plant, having something of the yellow water-lily and the deep marginals in its habit, is the fringed water-lily, *Limnanthemum nymphaeoides*, which has floating leaves and flowers of yellow with fringed petals which open cup-shaped and smell of almonds. These flower in July. It is mostly seen in pools and ditches in southern England and is of the same family as the bogbean, *Menyanthes trifoliata*, a plant for the shallow water at the side of a pond. In May and June, this bears large spikes of white and pink flowers, the petals being fringed on the inside with white hairs.

For marginal planting, either on the shelf or at the pond side, there are a number of lovely native plants, several delighting in having their roots entirely submerged, with anything up to 6in of water

E

above them. Of these, *Typha latifolia*, the false bullrush (almost always taken for the true bullrush) is conspicuous, with its dark brown spike 6in long, made up of hundreds of tiny flowers which are the females. They appear in July and August and do not fall until the spring. The lesser false bullrush, in bloom at the same time, has smaller spikes of paler brown with a space in the middle. Though the true bullrush, *Scirpus lacustris*, may in some circumstances attain a height of 7–8ft, it normally grows only 4–5ft tall, its flowers borne in terminal spikes of two or three, and its thick round leafless stems used for thatching and basketmaking. The flowers are small and oval and, when cut and dried, are useful for flower arrangement, but in no way do they resemble *Typha*. The spikelets are similar in their formation to those of the sea club-rush, *S maritimus*, which grows 3ft tall and is found in damp places near the coast. Here the spikelets are more closely clustered together whilst the thin leafy bracts extend above them.

The common spike rush, *S palustris*, grows to only half the height of *S maritimus* and bears its flowers in small terminal spikes from May to July. Increasing by underground stolons, it is frequently seen by the side of rivers and lakes, also in boggy ground.

The flowering rush, *Butomus umbellatus*, fairly widespread at one time by the side of water throughout England, but now less common due to land drainage schemes, is one of the most beautiful of our native plants, growing 3–4ft high, with a tuft of leaves at the top, like those of the crown imperial, but above which are a dozen or more pink flowers followed by purple fruits, each one held on a long footstalk. They are at their best from July until September. More confined to southern England, it is never found by stagnant water. It takes its botancial name from the Greek *bous*, 'an ox' and *temno*, 'to cut', for the sharp edges of the leaves will cut the mouths of grazing cattle. The seeds are slightly narcotic and countrymen would dry them and place them in muslin bags to inhale at bedtime as they were thought to induce sleep.

The arrowhead, *Sagittaria sagitifolia*, which grows to 2ft in height, its large arrow-shaped leaves held well above the water, is also a handsome marginal plant. The white flowers with their jet black centre, are borne in whorls on leafless stems and are most prominent during July and August.

At the side of the pool, plant the monkey flower, *Mimulus guttatus*,

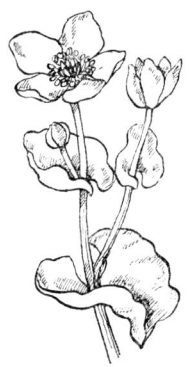

15 Marsh marigold

which grows less than 10in tall, its leaves stem-clasping, its deep-throated flowers of golden-yellow heavily spotted with red in the throat. The flower was so named because it is supposed to look like a monkey's face but I can never see the likeness. It is far more attractive than a monkey's face and is in bloom from June until September.

The marsh marigold, *Caltha palustris*, should be planted near it and, although it grows in damp places, I wonder if its name was originally 'March' marigold, for it comes into bloom during that month, and is colourful until June. Growing 20in tall, it has handsome rounded leaves, while the golden cup-shaped flowers, about 1in across, appear looking as if they have been varnished. There is also a lovely double form, *plena*.

The globe flower, *Trollius europeus*, more common in damp meadows on the Continent than the buttercup, but less common in Britain, is even more handsome than the marsh marigold. It grows rather taller, with deeply cut leaves, whilst the globe-shaped flowers of canary yellow are more than 1in across. These come into bloom about the first of June, just when the marsh marigold is beginning to fade and, with it, the greater spearwort, *Ranunculus lingua*, also begins to bloom. This plant needs to be on the marginal shelf for it likes to have its feet under several inches of water. It is a beautiful plant with large lanceolate leaves and bears its flowers, like large buttercups, at the end of 2ft stems. There is an improved form, *grandiflora*, which, as its name implies, bears flowers very much larger than the type.

The lesser celandine, *R ficaria*, Wordsworth's favourite flower which is carved on his tombstone, always does better in damp places than elsewhere, growing well in damp woodlands, ditches and damp meadows. With the primrose, it heralds the spring, for its dainty yellow flowers (nearly all the early wild flowers are yellow) appear with the first warm sunny days of March. When the sun is not shining, the flowers close up, to protect themselves from the impending rain. It grows only 3–4in tall and increases by small bulbils which form at the base of the leaf stalks.

With it may be found the water germander, *Teucrium scordium*, but this has become less prevalent in recent times, except in Ireland. A grey downy perennial, it bears its purple flowers in leafy whorls on 8in stems during July and August.

The yellow flag or water iris, *Iris pseudacorus*, is a plant for the marginal shelf or for the edge of a pond, for it likes to have its roots continually under water. It is a rhizomatous perennial with broad sword-like leaves, bearing golden-yellow flowers on a branched stem 3ft tall. The flowers are not bearded but have strikingly beautiful purple veins if seen close to, and an orange spot at the base of each petal. The plant is in bloom from May until August and there is a form with striking variegated foliage, the leaves being striped green and yellow, and one with lemon-coloured flowers, *bastardii*, which is equally lovely. As the fleur-de-lis, it was recognised as the emblem of France by Louis VII at the time of the Crusades.

The sweet flag, *Acorus calamus*, which provides us with the soothing calamine lotion, is of the *Arum* family, producing a spadix as its flower. This is made up of thousands of tiny yellowish-green flowers which are at their peak in July when they emit a most unpleasant smell. However, the stems, which reach a height of 5ft, and also the leaves, release a delicious fruity scent when crushed, likened by some to oranges, by others to ripe apples or lemons. In medieval times, the stems and leaves were in great demand for strewing on the floors of manor and church, being used to cover the floors of the great cathedrals of Ely and Norwich, as it was plentiful in the nearby Fenlands. In Canada, where the plant grows around the Great Lakes, the rhizomes are sliced and boiled in maple syrup to provide a tasty sweetmeat.

One of the few water umbellifers is *Oenanthe fistulosa*, the water dropwort, present in water meadows and marshy ground in the Midlands, often with its roots partially submerged. It grows 15in tall and forms its roots under water from the lower stem and nodes. The flowers are pinkish-white and appear in a domed head, making them more conspicuous to pollinating insects. They are at their loveliest in August and September and have with them the pleasing aroma of matured port.

The water figwort, *Scrophularia aquatica*, is an interesting and common plant of marshy ground. It grows 3ft tall and bears its maroon-coloured flowers with long footstalks, all the way up the stem. The flowers which are borne from June until September are followed by globular fruits.

The mints are also moisture-loving plants and grow well by the waterside, in ditches and in damp woodlands, for they are happy in partial shade. The smallest is pennyroyal, *Mentha pulegium*, its prominent lilac flowers appearing in a spike less than 4in tall. It is mostly confined to southern England and the east coast of Ireland and was once widely used for stuffing ducks or geese, hence its country name of pudding grass. Gerard tells us that it once grew in abundance at 'Mile End, near London' where it was sold in the streets to sweeten drinking water and to rid places of fleas. The royal palaces were numbered amongst its users, hence its name 'pulial-royal' which later became pennyroyal. Perhaps it sold for a penny a bunch.

Water mint, *M aquatica*, is much taller, reaching a height of almost 3ft, the toothed leaves releasing an orange-like scent when pressed. It is a handsome plant, with large reddish-purple flowers which are in bloom from July until September. The variety *crispa*, with curled leaves, is the chief source of oil of spearmint rather than *M spicata* itself.

Equally attractive is *M rotundifolia*, the round-leaf or apple mint which is widespread in deciduous woodlands and by the side of water in south west England and South Wales, though rare elsewhere. It grows 18in tall, the stems being covered in white hairs whilst the whole plant smells of ripe apples when pressed. The flowers are lilac-mauve and borne in cylindrical spikes. They are held on long foot-stalks whereas the flowers of most mints are borne at the leaf axils.

Present only in a few places, such as low-lying ground in Cambridgeshire and Bedfordshire, is the deliciously scented bergamot mint, *M citrata*, which releases the lemony scent of bergamot. A glabrous perennial with rounded heart-shaped leaves, the flowers are more reddish-purple than those of other mints. Indeed, when seen from afar, the whole plant takes on a purple hue.

The woodland mint, *M sylvestris*, its stems rising to a height of 2ft, is found under the same conditions, but is more widespread. The leaves are hairy on the underside which gives the plant a greyish appearance so that it associates admirably with *Stachys lanata* in the border.

Is there a lovelier plant than the meadowsweet, *Spirea ulmaria*? I do not think so. It is a plant equally at home in the wild garden as by the waterside. The Dutch rightly named it queen of the meadows and it was Queen Elizabeth's favourite plant for strewing in her apartments. When pressed or trodden upon, its leaves release a sharp aromatic scent, due to the presence of oil of wintergreen in its leaves, which Parkinson described as 'a pretty sharp scent'. He said that, 'a leaf or two laid in a cup of wine, will give as quick and fine a relish thereto as burnet will'. It takes its botanical name *ulmaria* from the Latin *ulmus*, 'an elm', because of the shape of its leaflets, and these impart their briskness to a pot pourri.

The water avens, *Geum rivale*, is a pleasing downy perennial herb, its leaves divided into three to six pairs of leaflets, whilst the small orange-pink flowers with their attractive reddish-brown sepals appear early in May. Though the plant is rare in the south, it is common about marshy ground in Scotland and northern England and at one time the roots, which have a hot clove perfume, were dried and used to make a nourishing tonic beer. The sliced roots, placed in wine or ale 'doth give it a delicate taste', so Culpeper tells us. In Canada, the roots are finely ground and used as a substitute for cocoa, drunk hot in winter.

The Himalayan balsam, *Impatiens glandulifera*, to be found by streams and lakes almost everywhere, is a colourful plant. I prefer its older name of water balsam, though it is also to be found on low-lying ground throughout the Near East and the Himalayas. It grows 4ft tall with pink stems and has few leaves, whilst the flowers are mauve-pink with a thin spur and hang down like a lantern. They appear from July until the end of summer.

Another bright and conspicuous balsam is the orange balsam, *I biflora*, which grows to a similar height, its orange flowers spotted with red and having a long spur, like the columbine. They are in bloom at the same time and usually appear in couples.

The columbine, *Aquilegia vulgaris*, grows well by the waterside and equally so in a border where the soil is well fortified with humus, enjoying moist, rather than wet, conditions. It is one of our most attractive wild flowers, the trifoliolate leaves having a greyish appearance, whilst the flowers are borne on 2ft stems and are, in Clare's words, 'of deep nightbrown'—though perhaps more navy-blue—and have long thin spurs which are more highly developed in the garden varieties. The flowers, which are visited by bees, have a drooping habit to shield the nectar. It seems to have no real culinary or medicinal value yet is one of the loveliest of wild flowers, in bloom during May and June. Known to countrymen as granny's bonnet or granny's bouret, its name is derived from the Latin *columba*, 'a dove', for the nectaries, like long spurs, are thought to resemble the head and neck of a dove. The poet Spenser compared his wife's neck 'like unto a bunch of collambynes' and in Elizabethan times, the flower came to be associated, like fennel, with flattery.

Yellow loosestrife, *Lysimachia vulgaris*, is a most colourful plant for a waterside garden. It has broad lanceolate leaves and bears its bright yellow flowers in leafy spikes at a height of 3–4ft. It is at its best during July and August. Before the age of mechanical transport, its presence was always welcomed by the weary traveller who would sit down close to it because it keeps flies away for quite a distance. Cottagers would cut the stems and hang them in the kitchen to keep flies away from food. The whole plant is covered in short hairs.

L nummularia, the creeping jenny of cottage gardens, does well in damp places. Also known as pennywort, the pale yellow flowers are bell-shaped and appear during June and July. Another species, *L thyrsiflora*, which grows 18in tall and is in bloom at the same time, bears dense leafy spikes of lemon-yellow flowers with prominent stamens. Making a compact tufted plant, it is quite often seen in damp woodlands and by lakes and ponds in northern England, but is now rare elsewhere.

The purple loosestrife, *Lythrum salicaria* (in no way connected to the yellow loosestrife), is an even more arresting plant with its tall spires of brilliant reddish-purple arranged all the way down the square stems, is often found by rivers and ponds, a mass of bloom during the midsummer months. Bees are regular visitors, working the flowers for nectar and pollen, the honey being dark with quite a rich flavour. This also makes an excellent border plant, growing 2–3ft tall and, of a number of garden varieties, the bright crimson beacon is outstanding.

The marsh mallow, *Althaea palustris*, a perennial growing 3–4ft tall, is strikingly lovely in leaf and bloom. Its broad-lobed leaves are greyish-green and soft and silky to the touch, whilst in late summer it bears soft pink cup-shaped flowers which measure more than an inch across. It is present throughout England and Wales, especially near the coast, on river estuaries and marshland. Taking its name from the Greek *althos*, 'a remedy', its root is sweet and mucilaginous, containing more than half its weight in saccharine mucilage, so that it is emollient, demulcent, soothing and lubricating. Gerard said that 'the leaves may be with good effect mixed with fomentations and poultices against pains of the sides; also in a bath they serve to take away all manner of pain'. From the roots, French druggists would prepare a delicious medicinal sweetmeat known as *pâté de guimauve* and, in France, the tender tops of the young shoots are used in salads.

A rare little plant, occasionally found in damp woodlands and by brooks and ponds in the north, is the marsh cinquefoil, *Potentilla palustris*. It is in bloom during May and June, bearing its rich mulberry-coloured flowers on 15in stems. They resemble those of the rock-rose and are of the same family, but the only one which enjoys some moisture about its roots, the other *Potentillae* requiring dry, sandy places. Again, the golden saxifrage, *Chrysosplenium oppositifolium*, is the only member of this family which prefers moisture and is often found near springs and other damp places. It is a prostrate perennial, with pale green leaves, bearing its small yellow flowers in a flattish head during April and May. It is pretty rather than showy.

Early spring is the best time to plant these waterside flowers. Plant them in small groups of two or three and about 18in apart. They are extremely hardy and long living and may be lifted and divided when the pool is cleaned, about every fifth year. Specialist growers of water plants stock most of them.

The Bog Garden

Where a pool is not required, most of the waterside plants such as *Caltha* and *Mimulus*, *Lysimachia* and *Lythrum* may be grown in an artificially made bog garden. Soil to the depth of 18in should be removed from the chosen site, leaving the sides gently sloping, and here those plants not requiring so much moisture about their roots should be grown.

The excavated area is lined with plastic sheeting, after removing any stones which might cause the sheeting to split under the weight of soil, and a mixture of peat and loam (equal parts by bulk of both) is put down. The area is then allowed several days to consolidate before planting. Afterwards, water is fed into the area by means of a hose connected to a length of pipe which reaches almost to the bottom of the bog garden, protruding just above the surface where it will be hidden by the plants. Sufficient water should be supplied to saturate the compost and whenever there is a period of dry, warm weather, additional water may be given. There must, however, be a continuous evaporation, for even the moisture-loving plants will not take kindly to having their roots in stagnant water, so during dull, wet weather, give little artificial moisture.

The plants will flourish under such conditions and soon spread out to form large clumps so that little soil will be seen. A more shaded part of the garden may be used for the bog garden for it will not be troubled by falling leaves which are so detrimental to a pond. Most of the plants will flourish in partial shade.

8

DELL AND SPINNEY

O blooming white narcissus-bud that lendest
New beauty to the meadow where thou bendest!

John Addington Symonds, *The Narcissus*

There is many a garden in which long-established trees with spreading
branches cast shade, beneath which little will grow. In other gardens
a small spinney could well be planted with native trees and shrubs,
with wild flowers requiring semi-shaded conditions which may also
be suitable to grow beneath trees of greater maturity. Among these
are primroses, cowslips, foxgloves and the common helleborine,
wood sage and ground ivy—plants enjoying similar conditions and
always at their best in a wild garden. All manner of flowering bulbs
may be grown too, and may be allowed to die back each year after
flowering, without any need to cut the grass which would quickly
reduce their vitality if the foliage was removed too soon. The plants
will seed themselves or, in the case of bulbs, will increase by underground bulbs and stolons.

It may be possible to fence off a corner of the garden and to keep
this in its wild state, creating a small woodland garden or spinney,
where silver birches with their strikingly beautiful bark may grow,
hazels with their catkins in early spring, the native flowering cherry,
hawthorn, and mountain ash with its trusses of red berries in autumn
and winter. All are native trees which grow well in various soils and
are handsome in flower and in fruit. While retaining their compact
habit, they will soon hide an unsightly vista from the house as well as
providing a tranquil corner for wildlife to enjoy as much as the
gardener.

Bulbous Plants for a Woodland Garden

Beneath the trees can be planted a bed of lily-of-the-valley, *Convallaria majalis*, its unique fragrance and ethereal beauty being unmatched by any other native flower. It requires a soil containing some leaf mould or decayed manure, retentive of summer moisture, and it loves the shade of valleys and woodland glades. Known to countrymen as the wood lily, Thomas Hill said that it was 'a marvellous sweet flower, flourishing in the springtime and growing properly in woods. But now . . . is brought and planted in our gardens', and writing in *The Flower Garden* (1726), John Lawrence said, 'The conval-lily is esteemed to have the sweetest and most agreeable perfume; not offensive or over-bearing, even to those who are made uneasy with the perfumes of other scented flowers.'

The manner in which the bells are suspended from the 6in stems gives them a daintiness possessed by few other flowers. The dark green sheathing leaf enhances the beauty of the white bells which are also tinted with green and are delightfully reflexed at the petal edges. There is a double form, too, *flore plena*, and one bearing pale pink flowers, both of which are occasionally seen in the wild, though neither are in any way lovelier than the type.

Another member of the lily family, is Solomon's seal, *Polygonatum multiflorum*, which bears its tiny white bells in two's and three's all the way along its 2ft stem and, like lily-of-the-valley, blooms in May and June. Its leaves, too, are borne all the way up the stem, hence its name 'ladder to heaven'. It should really be called 'Solomon's heal', for Dioscorides said that the roots, when dry and crushed and placed on wounds, caused them to heal quickly, and a writer of Elizabeth I's reign said that the roots 'stamped whilst fresh and green, and applied to the skin taketh away in one night any bruise gotten by woman's wilfulness in stumbling upon her hasty husband's fists'. The rhizomatous roots are best planted in November (as also are those of lily-of-the-valley), setting them just below the surface of the soil which should contain some peat or leaf mould.

Also of the lily family is the wild or woodland tulip, *Tulipa sylvestris*, which sends up its nodding yellow flowers, shaded green on the outside, to a height of 15in. Present in a few woodlands in northern England and across the Border, it blooms in April and May and in grass is a long-lived plant, whilst its flowers, which open star-like, are delightfully fragrant. With it and in the same areas grows the yellow star of Bethlehem, *Gagea lutea*, quite different from the true star of Bethlehem, but a delightful little plant in its own right, growing 4-5in tall, its yellow flowers being more like those of the lesser celandine, but with long strap-like leaves.

The common star of Bethlehem, *Ornithogalum umbellatum*, is found on grassy banks and in open woodlands in several parts of East Anglia. It grows 12in tall, the crocus-like leaves having a central white stripe whilst the white flowers, striped with green, are borne in quite a large umbel. Completely hardy, it flowers with freedom whether in a shrub border, short grass, or a wild garden, whilst the bulbs (which are planted in November, 3in deep and 4in apart) are quite inexpensive. This is the real star of Bethlehem, a native of Palestine which must have reached Britain with returning Crusaders, for it has been naturalised since earliest times. It is also present in Italy and there, as well as in Britain, the bulbs were used as food. Parkinson said that when roasted, they have a chestnut-like taste. The flowers last for many weeks in the garden and are equally long lasting when cut and placed in water.

O pyrenaicum, native of the Pyrenees has also been long naturalised here. During early Georgian times it was grown as a commercial crop around Bath, the unopened flower spikes being sold in bundles as 'Bath asparagus'. It is present in woodlands in the south west, the greenish-white flowers appearing on 2ft stems late in June when the star of Bethlehem has almost finished.

O nutans, the nodding star of Bethlehem is another lovely species and is the first to bloom, during April and May, forming an erect leafless scape of green and white striped bell-shaped flowers which open star-like and nod in the breeze. It is handsome in the garden and superb for flower arrangement. Plant the bulbs 3in deep and 8in apart.

Also present on grassy slopes near the sea in the south west is *Scilla verna*, the spring squill, which blooms from early April until June, bearing its dainty star-shaped flowers of porcelain blue on 4in stems. It looks lovely in pots in the home, also in troughs and in short grass whilst in the wild garden it should be planted 3in deep and 6in apart in bare ground beneath tall trees. Near it, plant the tubers of the winter aconite, *Eranthis hyemalis*. *Eranthis* is a Greek word meaning 'flower of the earth' and it is one of the best of all plants for growing beneath tall trees, once established it spreads rapidly, its golden chalices backed by an emerald green ruff which appears as the snow begins to melt. It is Thomas Noel's 'gloom-gilding aconite' and Gerard said 'it bloweth in January . . . yea, the colder the weather and deeper the snow, the fairer and larger is the flower'. Plant the tubers 3in apart and 2in deep, preferably in groups of a dozen or more for they are inexpensive.

In the short grass of mountainous slopes in several parts of north Somerset and the Cotswolds is to be found the grape hyacinth, *Muscari racemosum*, which blooms in April and May in a dense leafless spike. This rises to a height of 6in from several almost prostrate root leaves. The purple flowers resemble grapes rather than bells and have the delicious perfume of ripe plums. It is also known as the starch hyacinth, because the Elizabethans used the juice from the stems to stiffen their ruffs. Plant in October, 7–8cm bulbs 3in deep and 6in apart.

The bluebell or wild hyacinth is present in and along the sides of woodlands everywhere, but especially around Dovedale in Derbyshire and on the borders of Nottinghamshire and Staffordshire, its rich balsamic fragrance scenting the surrounding air during May and June. Indiscriminate pulling of the flowers, instead of cutting them and leaving a portion of stem to die back naturally so as to fortify the bulb for the following year, has caused a serious decline in bluebells in the woods around our industrial cities, as in the Eccleshall Woods near Sheffield and on Cannock Chase. Where less accessible, the bluebell, *Endymion nonscriptus*, casts a deep purple shadow beneath tall trees through which the sun's rays filter to present a picture of intense loveliness in early summer. The bells are held on 15in leafless stems which bend over at the tip, giving it a more fairy-like appearance than if the stems were entirely straight.

During Elizabethan times the bluebell was known as the harebell, whilst today the bluebell of Scotland is the flower we know in England as the harebell. To add to the confusion, the bluebell has changed its botanical name more often than any plant. Gerard knew it as the English hyacinth but in his day it was also known as the sea onion, for the bulbs were taken to sea by sailors, to be eaten as onions.

The flower is especially attractive seen against the white bark of the silver birch, but it may be planted almost anywhere in the wild garden. Plant the bulbs in autumn, 3in deep and 6in apart. They may readily be grown from seed sown ripe in July in boxes of John Innes compost. Place these in a frame for the winter and leave them for fifteen months, by when they will have formed quite large bulblets, suitable to plant out. They will come into bloom in another eighteen months. Alternatively, full-size bulbs can be obtained inexpensively from bulb merchants.

All bulbs will increase more rapidly if the dead flower heads are removed as they form. The bulbs will then also be more free flowering, for they will concentrate their energies on fortifying the bulb, rather than on forming seed.

Present in low-lying meadows in the Thames valley is *Fritillaria meleagris*, one of the most interesting of our wild flowers. It has grey grass-like foliage and in April and May bears, on a 6in stem, a solitary lantern-shaped bell, almost square and dull purple in colour with the outer surface divided into numerous chequered squares of darker purple—hence its old country name of the chequered daffodil; 'like the board at which men do play at chesse', wrote Gerard. It was also known as the ginny-hen flower, for from a distance it has the appearance of the feathers of a guinea fowl; and snakeshead fritillary, for the slightly drooping flowers with the purple and black markings greatly resemble the head of an adder, the squares of some flowers being green or pale yellow. It is ideal for orchard planting or a wild garden, provided the grass is not cut until the end of July. Plant the bulbs in autumn, 4in deep and 6in apart, preferably on a layer of peat or sand to assist drainage.

The meadow saffron, present in meadows over chalk or limestone, as in the Cotswolds and parts of east Yorkshire, Somerset and Wiltshire is another of our loveliest native plants and is one of the few bulbous plants to bloom in autumn. *Colchicum autumnale* is its botanical name, but far more descriptive is its country name of naked lady for it bears its rosy-mauve crocus-like flowers long before the leaves appear in early spring. They are long and broad and look untidy as they die back in summer so the plant is best confined to an orchard, shrubbery, or wild garden. From the long tuberous root or corm the drug colchicine is obtained, used by the ancients for gouty complaints, whilst modern science has discovered that it has the ability to increase the number of chromosomes in other plants, so that sterile hybrids can be made fertile. The whole plant is poisonous and should be kept away from grazing animals. Plant 20cm corms otherwise it will not bloom the first year, and plant in July when the foliage has died down. They should be planted 3in deep and 6–8in apart—handling the corms with care for there is a tube at the top through which the flower bud appears.

Meadow saffron is in no way connected with the autumn crocus with which it is so often confused. This latter is *Crocus nudiflorus* and is of the iris not the lily family. To add to the confusion it is also known as naked lady but it has more purple in its flowers and only three yellow stamens instead of six as in *Colchicum*. Plant the corms in summer, 4in deep. It increases by underground stolons, usually coming into bloom in its second year. Once established it is difficult to eradicate.

The native wild daffodil, *Narcissus pseudonarcissus*, is one of the most welcome of all our wild flowers. It is present in damp woodlands and meadows, chiefly in Warwickshire and Worcestershire, south into Devon, Dorset and Hampshire where it blooms during March and April. Its flowers are borne on a leafless scape and have a narrower trumpet and smaller perianth petals than the garden form, which adds to their charm. Perdita, in *A Winter's Tale*, has painted for us a delightful picture of the beauties of the Warwickshire countryside in springtime. It is significant that this was the first of Shakespeare's plays to be written after he had left London to take up residence at his New Place home at Stratford-on-Avon which he had purchased for his semi-retirement. He had returned to the countryside of boyhood days which he loved so well with the:

> Daffodils
> That come before the swallow dares, and take
> The winds of March with beauty

During Shakespeare's time, daffodils grew so profusely around London that each morning they were carried into the city by the women of Cheapside in large wicker baskets, balanced on their heads, to be sold for a penny a bunch. Known as Lent lilies, they were in bloom shortly before Easter and used to decorate the churches.

Plant the bulbs early in autumn, 3in deep and 6in apart, almost anywhere, although they prefer a good stiff loam to which some peat or leaf mould has been added. As with all bulbs, do not remove the foliage until the end of July when it has died down.

The pheasant's eye or poet's narcissus, a flower with a single round white perianth and small lemon-yellow eye, sometimes edged with red or green (like a pheasant's eye), has become naturalised in woodlands near several large towns, especially near Gravesend and Rochester in Kent. The flowers are sweetly scented and appear in April or May. Miss Sinclair Rohde, an authority on old flowers says their country name was sweet nancies, whilst Henry Lyte, translator of Dodoen's earlier work which he named the *New Herbal* (1578) called it 'the white primrose peerless'. Henry Phillips in the *Flora Historica* thought that this plant would most likely have come with the Romans for it is a common wild flower of Italy.

The origin of the Tenby daffodil, *Narcissus obvallaris*, is shrouded in mystery, but it may well be a native plant although it is seen only in a few meadows around Tenby in Wales. The flowers are deepest yellow, the trumpet being rather longer than that of *N pseudonarcissus*.

The Loddon lily, *Leucojum aestivum*, or summer snowflake, is found in meadows along the banks of the river Loddon and on the shores of the Shannon, flowering during the early weeks of summer. From a tuft of snowdrop-like leaves arises the 6in stem at the end of which twin flowers, or maybe as many as six, droop like snowdrops on thin footstalks. Indeed, they differ from snowdrops only in that their broader petals are equal in size. With snowdrops, the three inner segments are shorter than the three outer ones, but otherwise the plants are hardly indistinguishable. It makes a large bulb, like that of the daffodil.

L vernum, the spring snowflake, grows only half as tall, about 6–8in high, and blooms during February and March. It is a rare plant of a few shady woods in south-west England, its dainty white bells being tipped with green. Both require the same cool conditions as the snowdrop and a leafy humus-laden soil. Plant in autumn 3in deep and 6in apart.

The snowdrop, *Galanthus nivalis*, has always been a favourite with everyone, hence its many endearing country names such as

Plate 13 Angelica and other grey-leaved plants above a box hedge

Plate 14 Grape hyacinth,
Muscari racemosum

Plate 15 Meadow
saffron, *Colchicum
autumnale*

Candlemas bells, and milkflower from *gala*, 'milk', hence its botanical name. Gerard called it the bulbous violet, but when Johnson revised the *Herbal* in 1633 he named it the snowdrop, being the first to use the now familiar name. It enjoys cold conditions and so grows better in Northumberland and near the exposed east Yorkshire coast than in the south. It blooms early in January, being the first of the new season's flowers and it will come into bloom even if under a foot of snow. The white drooping bells are tipped with green and enhanced by a leafy hood which is an extension of the stem.

Snowdrops should be lifted, divided and replanted immediately after flowering, whilst the clumps are still green. Split them up into small pieces and plant 4in deep in a peaty soil. If planting bulbs, use the 3in size for if smaller they will take a year or more to bloom. Plant them 4in deep and 6in apart. There is also an attractive double form, *flore plena*.

The common cyclamen, *Cyclamen europeum*, found in mountainous regions across central Europe, is also a native plant, though now rare. Gerard has said that 'it groweth upon mountains in Wales and on the hills of Lincolnshire and Somerset (presumably the Quantocks)'. Today it is found in Kent and east Sussex. It is also *C hederifolium*, the ivy-leaf cyclamen of Elizabethan knot gardens and it bears the most sweetly scented flowers of all the hardy cyclamens whilst remaining in bloom from early July until late September. The purple-red flowers hover above the beautifully marbled leaves like butterflies.

The foliage is evergreen and acts as a pleasing foil for *Scilla verna* and snowdrops. Plant the large corms in April, with the smooth or rounded side downwards, 6in deep. They should be planted in leafy soil beneath mature trees where long grass cannot grow.

Shade-loving Plants

There are a number of plants which are not bulbous but which, like bulbs, grow better under shady conditions. Outstanding amongst these is the Christmas rose, *Helleborus niger*, which is not a native plant but has been naturalised in woodlands since earliest times and may have come with the Romans. It is the black hellebor, so called from the colour of its roots which were once used to treat mental disorders. Gerard said that 'a purgation of hellebor is good for mad and furious men . . . and those molested with melancholy'. The root

F

was dried and pounded, to be inhaled as snuff for the relief of headaches and moods of depression.

Also found in woodlands, usually growing in a limestone soil, in
the Cotswolds and as far north as Lincolnshire (where it grows in the
woodlands surrounding Grimsthorpe Castle), is the beautiful *H
viridis*, the green helleborine. One of the most valuable plants for the
flower arranger during winter and spring, it comes into bloom, in a
mild winter, at the beginning of the year, shortly after the Christmas
rose which it resembles in the shape of its flowers which are of the
same green colour as the leaves. Both grow 10–12in tall and may be
planted in the spinney and shrubbery provided the soil contains
plenty of leaf mould or decayed manure. Like the peony, they are
long-lived plants and may remain untouched for fifty years or more,
whilst each year they will provide more and more bloom. Plant them
18in apart and top dress in alternate years.

The stinking hellebore, *H foetidus*, is found under similar conditions but grows to 3ft in height. In March and April it bears clusters
of dull yellowish-green bell-shaped flowers above dark evergreen
palmate leaves. A handsome plant for a wild garden, it should not be
cut and used for indoor decoration for, when in bloom, it gives off a
most unpleasant smell, hence its familiar country name.

Anemone nemorosa, the wood anemone of the same buttercup family
as the hellebores, is a plant for shady places and is seen to advantage
planted in drifts in an orchard or in a wild garden or spinney. It may
also be planted in the shrub border, beneath early flowering cherries
and other spring-flowering trees and shrubs. If the ground is not dis-

16   Wood anemone

17   *Iris foetidissima*, the roast-beef plant

turbed, the plants will, in a few years, entirely cover the ground in the same way that *A nemorosa* forms a carpet of pure white flowers beneath the trees of deciduous woodlands. The flowers are borne solitary, on 6in stems, from March until the end of May. Sometimes the flowers are tinted with pink and the loveliest variety of all is *Robinsoniana*, named after the Victorian gardener, William Robinson, who discovered this beauty in his own garden at Gravetye Manor in Sussex. The flowers are of a gorgeous shade of silvery lavender-blue, enhanced by yellow anthers, and wherever it is seen, on the rock garden or beneath tall trees, it is the centre of attention. Plant the tubers 2in deep and 6in apart in October. They require a loamy soil containing plenty of peat or leaf mould.

Iris foetidissima, the roast-beef plant (so called because when the stems and evergreen leaves are crushed or cut, they release the not unpleasant smell of beef cooking on a spit), is also present in chalky woodlands, producing in June and July its purple-grey irises in dense tufts on 2ft stems. The flowers are followed by long vivid-green fruits which split to reveal, in the dark November days, rows of vermilion-coloured seeds which are most striking when used for indoor decoration.

Growing with it may be found the wood spurge, *Euphorbia amygdaloides*, an unbranched perennial some 15in tall with narrow, bright green leaves. The dull yellow flowers, which are borne from March until May, are held on 2in long footstalks in terminal clusters, making this, also, an excellent flower for indoor decoration. *E virgata* is similar and though thought to be an introduction, has now become more common than the wood spurge and is found in shady lanes and deciduous woodlands in many parts of southern England, flowering during June and July to extend the display. Both species are perennial and should be planted 2ft apart.

Often found with them, for it enjoys the same soil and climatic conditions, is the interesting perennial, herb Paris, *Paris quadrifolia*, which releases an unpleasant foetid smell when handled, yet is a delightful plant for the wild garden. It grows 12in high and, at the top of the otherwise leafless stem, has four broad grey-green leaves which terminate in a point. In May, from the centre the green flower appears with four narrow petals and four green sepals. The plants like a soil containing plenty of leaf mould to retain summer moisture.

Always a delight to come upon in woodland or leafy hedgerow is the ground ivy, *Glechoma hederacea*. A labiate, it is an almost prostrate perennial, but may be used in hanging baskets and window boxes where it will send down its grey-green trailing shoots to a distance of several feet. It may also be used to cover a bare shady bank which it will do entirely if several are planted 12in apart. Its hairy heart-shaped leaves are deliciously aromatic when pressed, whilst from April until July it bears whorls of purple-blue flowers in the axils of the leaves. It propagates with the greatest ease, forming roots at the leaf joints as the stems trail along the ground. Pieces may then be detached and planted in small pots or into the open ground. Gerard, who was born in Nantwich, said that the people of North Wales and Cheshire would place the leaves in mugs of ale to clarify it, before the advent of hops—hence its north-country name of ale-hoof. The leaves were also used to make a 'tea' to purify the blood. The plant takes its name from the Greek, *glechon*, 'mint', and under a microscope the essential oil, with its minty smell, may be seen exuding from the glandular dots on the undersurface of the leaves.

Another labiate, and one of the loveliest of our woodland flowers, is the wood sage, *Teucrium scorodonia*, which is often found massed, the plants growing about 2ft high with wrinkled, oval grey-green leaves, like those of the common sage. The dull yellowish-green flowers are borne in leafy spikes in one-sided clusters but are made more noticeable to pollinating insects by their wine-red stamens. Though the flower tube is about 10mm long, so much nectar is secreted during July and August that it reaches halfway up the tube and so is available to honey bees which work the flowers freely. Although truly perennial, it usually behaves like a biennial, seeding itself and flowering the following year. The foxglove, *Digitalis purpurea*, is essentially a woodland or wild garden plant, growing to a height of 3–4ft and bearing its 2in long tubular purple flowers from June until summer ends. The flowers are borne all along the stem and are shaped like the fingers of a glove. Abraham Cowley wrote of

> The foxglove on fair flora's hand is worn,
> Lest while she gathers flowers, she meets a thorn.

But where the 'fox' part comes in, no one seems to know. When the flowers advance from the calyx they are tightly closed by the four clefts of the corolla so that air cannot enter until the parts of fructification have reached maturity. The lips then part to form a trumpet which remains open for several days, until the anthers have discharged their farina, when the trumpet falls away to enable the sun to ripen the seed. For the plant to be long living, it is necessary to cut away the stem to 6–8in above the ground so that it will not use up its energies in the production of large quantities of seed.

Plants are easily raised from seed sown in summer and may be removed to their flowering position the following spring, to bloom in July. Plant 15in apart and in generous groups to see them to advantage.

There are two species of forget-me-not that are widespread in damp woodlands and by the side of woodlands. Bearing masses of tiny flowers of brilliant blue, from March until July, they may also be planted in beds together with spring-flowering daffodils and other wild flowers. They are slightly hairy perennials—mostly treated as biennials, where used for bedding, sowing the seed in June in drills and transplanting to their flowering quarters in early autumn to bloom the following spring. The common forget-me-not, *Myosotis arvensis*, grows 6in tall with leaves shaped like a mouse's ears (hence its botanical name), bearing its blue flowers in forked spikes. The flowers of *M sylvatica*, the wood forget-me-not, are of a clearer and paler blue and almost twice the size. Both plants have been used in raising modern hybrid varieties, amongst the best of which are blue ball and ultramarine, forming compact plants 6–8in tall. They are most attractive when planted with yellow cowslips or primroses.

The flower was taken by Henry of Lancaster, later Henry IV, as his emblem in the belief that whoever should wear it would never be forgotten. Yet it was first named forget-me-not by the poet Coleridge in *The Keepsake* in which he writes of,

> That blue and bright-eyed floweret of the brook,
> Hope's gentle gem, the sweet forget-me-not.

Like the forget-me-not, the yellow and purple loosestrifes are also equally at home by water as in damp woodlands; also the willow-herbs of which *Epilobium hirsutum*, the great willowherb is the most colourful. It grows 4–5ft tall and has long hairy leaves which are stem-clasping, whilst the purple-pink flowers are borne in terminal cymes during August and September.

The common helleborine, *Epipactis helleborine*, is very handsome. An orchid, it produces its flower spike from July until September at a height of about 18in, its leaves alternating along the stem. The flowers resemble those of the wood sage and are yellowish-green, produced in a one-sided spike. The sepals terminate to a point, whilst the lip is without any spur. These have no perfume, but the green-winged orchid, *Orchis morio*, is deliciously fragrant. It grows to about 9in and is quite common in woodlands and often in meadows and downlands, the spurred flowers ranging in colour from deep purple to white. It is distinguished from the early purple orchid by green veins in the hooded sepals. It blooms in May and June. With it blooms O *maculata* which may also be raised from seed, but requires an acid soil, so dig in plenty of peat. The seed should also be germinated in coarse peat or in sphagnum moss. Once established, it thrives on competition and is long living, producing pale pink flowers with spreading sepals on leafy stems 18in tall. The flowers are usually dotted with crimson.

9

PLANTS FOR THE SHRUB GARDEN

... the slowe-thorn white,
As if a flaky shower the leafless sprays
Had hung; the hawthorn, May's fair diadem;
The whin's rich dye; the bonny broom; the rasp
Erect; the rose, red, white and faintest pink;
And long extending bramble's flowery shoots.

James Grahame, *Scotland*

It is not generally realised how many of our native shrubs are suitable for inclusion in borders, whilst many are valuable for planting in the shaded garden, amongst these being the spurge laurel, berberis and viburnum. The wild privet, one of the loveliest of our native flowers is also tolerant of partial shade, whilst the hawthorn and blackthorn are seen to advantage in hedgerow and woodland.

A shrub border can be formed entirely with native plants, including several of our smaller trees such as the flowering crab and wild cherry, especially the double-flowering variety which is one of the best of all small garden trees. They may be planted at the back of a shrub border to hide a screen of interwoven or ranch-type fencing, with the more compact shrubs to the front. Such small trees will give height to a shrub border and beneath them wild-flower bulbs may be planted which can be left to increase each year, as in the wild garden, from underground bulblets and from seed. Against the fence, dog roses and sweet briar may be grown, or their long sturdy stems may be tied to strong wires stretched across a fence at intervals of about 18in. These roses will make an impenetrable fence or hedge if the stems are tied to wires fastened to wooden posts which are fixed into the ground at intervals of 8ft, and used to separate the gardens of a semi-detached house, or a garden from a public footpath. Alternatively, against a trellis fence, which may be used to divide one part of the garden from another, grow blackberry plants which will give fruit in autumn when the leaves turn a brilliant golden-yellow colour.

The honeysuckles and traveller's joy may also be planted to form a screen. They can be used at the back of a shrub border, growing them against stakes 6ft above ground and spaced out in tent fashion, or planting one in a circle of wire netting held in place by a strong post. As twining plants, they will soon pull themselves up the stakes or netting and will climb 5–6ft in a year, almost entirely hiding the supports. Plant them about 8ft apart in the border with possibly a crab or cherry tree between them.

To the front of those 'back cloth' trees, plant taller-growing shrubs such as the tree lupins and tamarisk, gorse and broom, elder and buddleia, each of which need an open, sunny situation to give of their best but which are normally happy in dry, gravelly soil. It is surprising how adaptable most plants are and in my spinney garden, on the side facing due west, the brooms bear an abundance of flower that I have not seen matched elsewhere. The plants are protected from the north-east winds and, being partially shaded by overhanging trees, retain their blossom for weeks on end, their brilliant gold colouring making a striking picture against the sombre green stems, especially when set alight by the setting sun. Yet for long it has been established that broom cannot be expected to perform well under such conditions, requiring an aspect open to the midday sun. In front of these, plant the daphne and St John's wort, the berberis and sweet gale.

Making a Shrub Border

A shrub border requires the same attention as the herbaceous border in its preparation, for it is of little use planting into weed-infested ground which will choke the plants before they become established. The border should be made at least 6ft wide and can be of any length. It may be made in a half-moon shape or, on the side edged by a lawn, it may be of gently undulating lines.

After marking it out with a garden line, dig over the ground two spits deep, removing all perennial weeds such as docks and nettles, as the work continues. If the ground is badly drained, work in some crushed brick or rubble and any materials of humus value such as peat or shoddy, decayed manure and clearings from ditches. Give the soil a 2oz per square yard dressing of bone meal as the work continues and, after allowing the soil several days to consolidate, plant when it is in a friable condition. Most plants are readily obtainable from nurserymen but many may be raised from seed sown in April in boxes or pans containing a John Innes compost, covered by glass. Place in a sunny corner outdoors, or in a cold frame, and grow on the seedlings in small pots until the following spring when they should be planted in the border. The brooms, gorse, tree lupins, sweet gale and St John's wort are all readily raised from seed, but the double gorse is propagated from cuttings, as are the privet, elder and the thorns. These will, in fact, grow readily from seed, but will take longer to reach planting size.

Always plant firmly and not too close together. Even those of most compact habit will soon spread out to cover an area of at least 1sq yard which must be the minimum of ground allowed for each plant. If shrubs are planted too close they will grow into each other, causing those parts of the plant to die back through lack of sunlight and air. Plants grown in containers may be planted throughout the year, except when frost is in the soil. After planting, they will require little attention, although all shrubs appreciate a mulch of garden compost or decayed manure and peat. This may be applied at almost any time, supplying the plants with nourishment and keeping the roots cool in summer, whilst helping to retain moisture during hot weather.

Small Trees for a Border
The bird cherry, *Prunus padus*, is a small tree or shrub with dark

18   Bird cherry

brown bark which, when removed, releases a pungent smell, The flowers, which are white and borne in drooping racemes of twenty or more, have a sweet almond-like perfume which is absent from the double form, *cerasus rhexii*, but which is one of the loveliest of the May-flowering cherries. Gerard told us that the wild cherry grew in Westmorland and in Lancashire where it was to be found 'almost in every hedgerow'. It is a valuable plant to use as a windbreak in exposed positions and grows particularly well in calcareous soils.

The crab apple, *Malus sylvestris* (syn: *Pyrus malus*), is also common in hedgerows about England and Wales and makes a small deciduous tree with grey bark. The flowers are white, tinted pink or crimson and have attractive golden anthers. They are at their loveliest in May and early June and are followed by small round yellow apples, striped with red, which may be used to make a delicious jelly or conserve. In Elizabethan times, the apples were sliced and put in ale to bring out the fullness of its flavour. In *Love's Labour's Lost* Shakespeare's 'When roasted crabs hiss in the bowl' refers to the custom of first roasting the apples before putting them into ale. From the wild crab a number of choice varieties have been raised, including John Downie which makes a neat upright tree with white flowers made more colourful in autumn with its golden-orange egg-shaped apples which are amongst the best for making conserve. Goldsworth red is equally attractive, the white flowers being followed by crimson fruits which, if not required for making jelly, hang until the New Year.

For a hedge, or to grow as a specimen tree in the standard form, the May or hawthorn, *Crataegus monogyna*, with its three to seven lobed leaves and greyish-white flowers smelling much like herring brine, is outstanding, for it makes dense growth and comes early into leaf and is one of the last trees to lose its foliage. It is considered unlucky to take the flowers indoors, and the unpleasant smell of decaying fish is due to the presence of trimethylamine, present also in the early stages of putrefaction. Those of *C oxyacanthoides*, which are creamy-white with pink anthers, have a similar smell and are followed by small crimson fruits which, like those of May, make a syrup which is rich in vitamin C. This species is always found in woodlands, rarely in hedgerows.

The blackthorn is *Prunus spinosa*, an upright thorny shrub growing 8–10ft tall, its young twigs covered in grey down whilst the pure white flowers appear early in spring, before the leaves. With age, the twigs take on a jet black appearance which accentuates the whiteness of the flowers and these are followed by purple-black fruits known as sloes, used in the making of a gin.

Even earlier flowering is *P cerasifera*, the cherry-plum, which has larger flowers than the blackthorn and twigs free from down. The fruits are yellow, tinted with crimson and have no value for any purpose.

Of the same family is the mountain ash, *Sorbus aucuparia*. It has small creamy-white flowers borne in a corymbose cyme of thirty or more and having the same unpleasant scent as *Crataegus monogyma*. They are followed by red, orange or yellow fruits (berries) which, in autumn, present a handsome sight against the dark fern-like leaves before they fall. *S aucuparia* is a deciduous tree growing 20ft tall, but is ideal for the small town garden and grows well in the poorest of soils.

Also making a tree of similar height is the white beam, *S aria*, its toothed leaves being silvered on the underside, whilst its cymes of creamy-white flowers appearing in May are followed by bunches of crimson berries. It is widely distributed in chalk or limestone soils.

Another garden tree of limited proportions is *S terminalis*, the wild service tree, the twigs and leaves being downy on the underside. It bears large flat heads of creamy-white flowers in May and June followed by trusses of handsome red berries.

The Wild Roses

Of our wild roses, the commonest is the dog rose, *Rosa canina*, its large thorns being shaped like a dog's canine teeth. One of the longest living of all plants, its roots are almost indestructible and it sends out its thick prickly stems to 10ft or more. The flowers appear in June and July and measure 2in across. They are of soft pink with golden stamens and are followed by large round crimson seed capsules, hips, which are rich in vitamin C. The syrup can be used as a substitute for orange juice in winter. Of rose-hip jelly, Culpeper said that it 'maketh most pleasant meats and banqueting dishes' and Gerard wrote that for 'tarts and such like ... I commit to the cunning cook.'

The single dog rose is the heraldic rose, usually shown with the green 'leaves' (calyx) appearing between the petals. It figures in the arms of the town of Montrose, Scotland.

The sweetbriar or eglantine, *R rubiginosa*, is widespread in the Cotswolds and across southern England from Kent to Dorset, but rare elsewhere. Found mostly in hedgerows, it forms a dense erect bush, its graceful arching stems clothed in hooked spines whilst its downy leaves are covered in small brown glands on the underside, which, when pressed (or after a heavy shower), release a refreshing fruity scent, like that of ripe apples. The flowers, which are borne three or four together, are deepest pink and are followed by vivid scarlet pear-shaped hips which are retained well into winter. Two distinctive forms make admirable garden plants—one, Janet's pride, was discovered in a Cheshire hedgerow in 1892, its deep pink flowers having a contrasting white centre; and the double scarlet, which bears flat semi-double blooms of glowing red.

The field or musk rose, *R arvensis*, is also common in hedgerows throughout England and Wales, but mostly south of a line from the Wash to the Dee, being less common in the north and extremely rare in Scotland and Ireland. Shakespeare coupled the 'sweet musk rose', a familiar plant of the Warwickshire countryside, with the eglantine to provide the canopy beneath which Titania slept, and Francis Bacon included it amongst those flowers 'yielding the sweetest smell in the air'. One of the last of our wild roses to bloom, coming in July and August, it bears its honey-scented white flowers with reflexed purple sepals solitary, and also in two's and three's.

Present on sand dunes and in coastal districts in western Scotland and in Ireland is *R spinosissima*, the burnet or Scottish rose, which spreads by means of underground suckers to form a dense thicket.

19   Burnet rose

The stems which grow to a height of 2–3ft are covered in long spines whilst the creamy-white flowers are borne solitary and without bracts. They have a delicious fruity perfume and appear from mid-May until July, to be followed by blackish-crimson hips. A variety found at Falkland in Scotland and bearing that name has greyish foliage and bears semi-double flowers of palest pink.

Of the same family is the yellow cinquefoil, *Potentilla erecta*, which grows to 2ft in height and bears its primrose-yellow flowers in generous clusters during July and August. The flowers, which are about 1in across, are produced in clusters on erect stems which makes this a suitable plant for a small border. In the wild it is found on railway banks and similar quite inaccessible places.

Plants of Climbing Habit

Suitable to cover a trellis or to grow in 'tents' at the back of a border is *Clematis vitalba* which, in Gerard's time, was to be found in every hedgerow from Gravesend to Canterbury. Weary travellers could rest in its shade, 'whereupon', wrote Gerard, 'I have named it traveller's joy'. It has woody stems and climbs by the twisting petioles of the leaves. Its vanilla-scented, greenish-white flowers are borne at the axils of the leaf stems during July and August. They are without true petals, their place being taken by four sepals, whilst there are many stamens. The fruit is an achene with long feathery styles, like white plumes, which persist through winter and from which the plant takes its other name of old man's beard.

The two honeysuckles of our hedgerows and woodlands should be in every wild-flower garden for they may be grown (with *C vitalba*) against an old tree trunk or on a trellis. They are also at their best planted against a rustic arch which is used as an entry point for a part of the garden.

Lonicera periclymenum, the woodbine, is a native plant with richly-scented flowers of creamy-yellow appearing throughout summer. *L caprifolium* is native to southern Europe but was introduced early in our history and has for long been naturalised in southern England. It is distinguished from the native species in that its upper leaves are united at the base whilst the creamy-white flowers, conspicuous at night, are borne in whorls. They have the corolla-tube extended so that they are fertilised only by night-flying lepidoptera—hence they are scented only at night—whilst those of *L periclymenum* are scented both by night and day.

These climbing plants, tolerant of partial shade, grow well in ordinary garden loam, but *Clematis vitalba* requires a soil containing a little mortar or lime rubble. As with all plants for the shrubbery, they are best set out in November, though where raised from seed, early spring is a more suitable time.

Some Handsome Native Shrubs

Of the same family are the *Viburnums*, amongst the loveliest of all our native plants, deciduous shrubs growing 10–12ft tall and present in woodlands and hedgerows, mostly in south-east England, East Anglia and east Yorkshire, always being more abundant in calcareous soils. *Viburnum lantana* with its dark-green heart-shaped leaves, serrated at the edges, bears its scented creamy-white flowers in a flat-topped umbel during May and June. It received its country name of the way-faring tree as its leaves provided dense shade during the heat of summer.

The guelder rose, *V opulus*, has five-lobed leaves which, in autumn, take on rich shades of yellow, bronze and crimson. The white flowers are borne in flat umbels and are at their best during July and August when those of *V lantana* are finishing. The outer flowers of each umbel are sterile, with petal-like corollas; the inner flowers being followed by vivid scarlet fruits.

Though it has few friends, the elder is handsome both in bloom and in fruit. Its appearance on waste ground and the unpleasant smell of its bark tend to make it unpopular for garden planting, yet it takes its name from the Norse, *Hulda*, goddess of love, and in northern Europe it is held to be sacred. In the garden, it will reach a height of 20ft. When warmed by the sun, its creamy-white flowers, borne in flat-topped cymes, emit a musky perfume. In France, the flowers are laid on racks or benches and early apples and pears placed over them to absorb their muscatel flavour. Elderberry wine, made from the ripe fruit is delicious when taken hot at bedtime. Cobbett wrote: 'a cup of mulled elder, with nutmeg and sippets of toast, just before going to bed on a cold wintry night, is a thing to be run for'.

For winter colour, *Cotoneaster simonsii* has for so long been natura-lised that it has come to be included amongst our native plants. With its neat upright habit, it may be grown against a bare wall, or as a hedge, as well as being a colourful member of the shrub border, for it is evergreen and has orange berries which turn crimson in winter.

Those several members of the barberry family, native to Britain or long naturalised here, should be included in every shrub garden. They are evergreen and grow in shade, their handsome glossy leaves being sharply toothed or pointed. The native *Berberis vulgaris* grows to a height of 6ft in a rich loamy soil and in early summer bears drooping clusters of bright lemon-yellow flowers, followed by red oblong fruits from which a delicious preserve can be made. The flowers are much visited by bees.

The closely related *Mahonia aquifolium*, native of the western states of America and long naturalised here, is now more common than the native *Berberis* which is known to harbour the 'rust' disease which attacks wheat. Its glossy leaves make it admirable for cutting to use with spring flowers, while making a dense bush, 3ft tall, it is widely planted for game coverts. Its panicles of yellow flowers, which appear in March, have the lily-of-the-valley perfume and are followed by quite large black grape-like fruits covered in white 'bloom'.

A plant of similar habit, though deciduous, is sweet gale, *Myrica gale*, also known as bog myrtle. It grows to 3ft tall and is found about low-lying heathlands, so, if planting in the garden, work plenty of peat into the soil. The flowers are catkins, borne in April, the orange male and crimson female appearing in separate plants. The whole plant, the reddish stems and grey-green leaves are covered in pellucid dots which release a sweet resinous scent when pressed. It is a handsome plant in all respects but does not do well in limestone soils which so well suit the barberries.

A plant for all shrub borders and, like the barberries happy in semi-shade, is the common St John's wort, *Hypericum perforatum*, an evergreen perennial growing 2–3ft tall. The small oblong leaves are dotted with pellucid glands which release the rather unpleasant smell of wet fur when handled. Its handsome golden flowers are borne from July until September. To the ancients it was a holy herb, the red sap of the stems and leaves being believed to represent the blood of John the Baptist so that it was thought to have more medicinal properties than any other plant. An infusion of the leaves was used to ease a hard cough and to prevent young children from bed-wetting, whilst an ointment prepared from these leaves and olive oil is still used to treat bed-sores.

The sweet amber or tutsan, from the French *toute-saine*, 'all heal' (so called because of the antiseptic properties of its oval evergreen leaves), is a handsome sub-shrub, growing 3ft tall. It is present in damp shady woodlands in south-west England and South Wales. *H androsaemum* bears amber-coloured flowers in July, in bunches of five, followed by purple-black fruits. The leaves and stems retain their camphoraceous smell after drying and may be placed amongst clothes and bedding to deter moths.

The rose of Sharon, *H calycinum*, an evergreen undershrub growing 1–2ft tall, is a most handsome plant in all respects. Several, planted together 2ft apart, will soon hide the ground with their oval leaves of brightest green, whilst its yellow flowers of at least 3in in diameter, are amongst nature's finest treasures. A bunch of stamens with red anthers can be seen in the midst of each of its flowers which appear in long succession from June until the end of August.

It is not generally realised that the common privet, *Ligustrum vulgare*, is a member of the same family as the lilac although in inhaling its flowers something of the same perfume can be detected, but with fishy undertones due to the presence of trimethylamine. In bloom, the privet possesses a beauty never seen in the clipped plant used as a hedge. The plant, which grows 10–12ft tall, is evergreen and in June and July creamy-white flowers are borne in large panicles like those of the lilac, enhanced by the dark green foliage. These are followed in autumn by shiny black fruits from which a distilled water was obtained to use as a mouth wash for ulcers. The privet grows well in ordinary soil, but especially over limestone.

The closely related *Buddleia davidii*, although a plant of eastern Asia, has become so widely naturalised on waste land that it is now included with our native plants. It grows 6–7ft tall with arching cane-like stems, and has grey-green lanceolate leaves. The flowers are borne from July to September and are lilac-pink, formed in dense narrow panicles. When warmed by the sun, they have a honey-like perfume and are frequently visited by butterflies which extract the nectar from the long tubes of the flowers. From this plant several colourful varieties have been raised, including black knight, deep purple; white bouquet; and Glasnevin blue. Ordinary soil is all it

Plate 16 The privet, *Ligustrum vulgare*. When allowed to grow freely, the privet bears a profusion of heavily scented white blooms.

Plate 17 The flowers of the common elder, *Sambucus nigra*

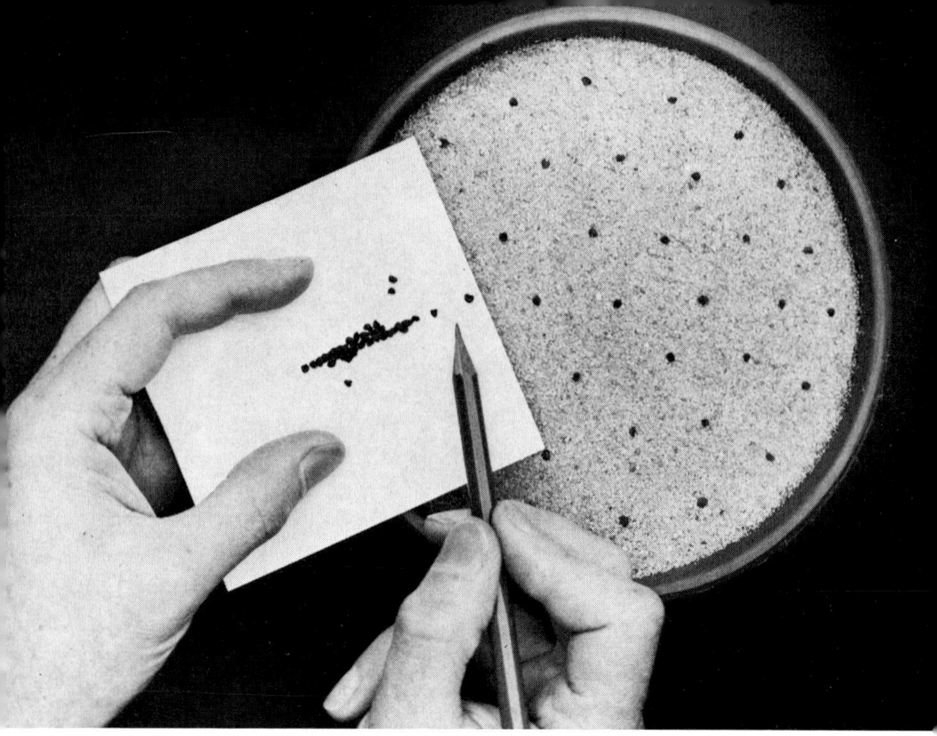

Plate 18 Spacing seeds. The seeds are held on a sheet of paper and a pencil is used to push them singly onto the compost

Plate 19 Seedlings are watered from the bottom of the compost by carefully holding the pan in a shallow bowl of water

requires and it is best pruned hard back each year in early spring. It is a hardy and fast-growing plant.

Several members of the pea family, including the gorse, broom and tree lupin are admirable plants for a shrubbery. The gorse, *Ulex europeus*, is so common on dry banks everywhere that it is rarely planted in gardens, but in good soil grows 8ft tall and blooms almost all year. Its spines are its leaves and the golden pea-like flowers have wings longer than the keel. They emit a refreshing fragrance like that of ripe oranges or pineapples. The seeds are contained in green pods which, when they ripen in autumn, 'pop' as they open, as William Hewitt wrote:

> The crackling of the gorse flowers near,
> Pouring an orange-scented tide
> Of fragrance o'er the desert wide.

The double-flowered form, *flore plena*, is the best for gardens, its dark green stems being covered in double golden flowers for weeks on end, but especially during spring and early summer.

The broom, *Cytisus scoparius*, is like a gorse without spines and is more willowy. Readily grown from seed, sown one to a small pot in April, it will in two years have made a dense bush as wide as it grows tall (about 6ft). It blooms from May until August, bearing its unscented but striking golden flowers in one's and two's. It does not grow well on chalk or limestone soil and will die back if clipped when it has once become established. Any pruning must be done in the first two years.

The tree lupin, *Lupinus arboreus*, like the buddleia, is a native of East Asia, but has become naturalised on old walls and embankments almost everywhere. It, too, is readily raised from seed and will quickly make a dense bush 3ft tall, its palmately divided leaves being evergreen, whilst during June and July it provides a wealth of small lupin-like spikes of primrose-yellow. It grows well in the poorest soil but, like the broom, will not transplant unless in the seedling stage. There are white and mauve varieties but neither are as attractive as the type.

The tamarisk, *Tamarix anglica*, is a graceful evergreen which grows 8–10ft tall and always does well in a sandy soil and close to the sea. It has feathery lace-like foliage and reddish stems, bearing its soft pink

G

flowers in cascading plumes in July and August. A handsome hybrid variety is pink cascade, bearing deeper pink flowers in larger plumes. This plant dislikes moving except when young and, like the broom, also resents clipping when once established.

Found only in isolated places near the sea in Southern Ireland, but, for all that, native to these islands, is the strawberry tree, *Arbutus unedo*, an evergreen growing 6–7ft and ideal for small gardens where the soil is of a limestone nature. Its trunk has handsome reddish bark and it bears clusters of lily-of-the-valley-shaped flowers at the same time as the large round fruits which are edible and take two years to mature. To have fruit, plant in pairs for cross-pollination. It is a member of the heath family, most of which require soil of an acid nature and, apart from the Cornish heather, will not grow in limestone. Most heathers will grow in ordinary soil, however, provided plenty of peat is packed about the roots when planting. They may be grown at the front of a shrub border or in small alpine beds by themselves, to provide rich patches of colour almost throughout the year.

The Cornish heather, *Erica vagans*, found growing about the rocks of the Lizard peninsula, is evergreen and makes a large, thick bush 2–3ft tall. From July to September it bears lilac-pink flowers with conspicuous brown anthers in long crowded spikes. Lyonesse bears white flowers with the same conspicuous anthers, whilst Diana Hornibrook bears spikes of deep coral-red.

The other native heathers require an acid soil. Of these, the Irish heath, *E hibernica*, is to be seen in the wet bogs of the west coast of Ireland where, in the mild, moist climate it may reach a height of 5ft, the pale mauve flowers appearing in April and May, borne in a leafy spike. There is also a white form, *alba*. These should be grown along the western side of Britain for they are less hardy than other heaths.

There are several outstanding varieties of the common ling, *E vulgaris*, present on moorlands everywhere, colouring them with its purple and mauve flowers during the mellow weeks of autumn. Golden feather has brilliant golden foliage whilst Goldsworth crimson bears contrasting flowers of deep red. Plant near it the double white heather, *alba plena*, and H. E. Beale, with its curved spikes of a glorious shade of silvery lilac-pink, the flowers being fully double. These heathers grow 18in tall.

E cinerea is found about the same terrain, but is in bloom two months earlier. It grows 18in tall and makes a bushy evergreen shrub, its stems covered in tiny crimson-purple bells. The variety C. D. Eason is of deeper crimson-red, whilst *alba* bears pure white flowers contrasting with the dark green foliage.

The Dorset heath, *E ciliaris globosa*, bears pink oval-shaped flowers on an erect spike from June until October. *E tetralix mollis* is the handsome silvery-grey cross-leaf heath, growing 10in tall, its stems crowned with clusters of tiny white flowers. The variety *darleyensis* bears bright pink flowers.

The closely related *Pyrola minor*, the wintergreen, is a gem for the alpine garden, a short spike of pinkish-white bells arising from a rosette of round dark green leaves during July and August.

The two daphnes, *Daphne mezereum* and *D laureola*, the spurge laurel, are most pleasing under-shrubs for a shady border, both growing about 2ft tall though taking a considerable time to do so. Both daphnes are found in damp deciduous woodlands and, as they grow best in a limestone soil, are most often found in copses and spinneys in the Cotswolds and Chiltern Hills. *D mezereum*, a favourite plant of old cottage gardens is deciduous, its spikes of fragrant pinkish-purple flowers appearing in February, before the leaves. One is tempted to cut the shoots to allow them to open indoors so that they will scent a large room but, if done too often, this will cause the plant to die back. The spurge laurel is evergreen, its long glossy dark green leaves being like those of the laurel while, at the end of the shoots, are numerous pale green flowers of powerful fragrance which appear in March and April.

10

THE HERB GARDEN

The pleasant way, as up those hills you climb,
Is strew-ed o'er with marjoram and thyme,
Which grows unset.

George Withers, *A Poet's Home*

The flowers of most plants grown for their scented leaves are usually insignificant, yet their interesting foliage should guarantee them a place in every wild-flower garden. These plants may form a small herb garden for their leaves will have many uses throughout the year. They may be used in the kitchen, to add interest to meatless dishes, to omelettes and salads; and also in sweet bags and pot pourris to place amongst clothes and linen or beneath a pillow to induce sleep, the scent being released by the pressure of the head upon the pillow and warmth of the body. They may also have value in easing simple complaints like a head cold or sore throat.

To Make a Herb Garden

Select an open, sunny situation. Herbs must have sunlight to bring out the full fragrance of their leaves. Apart from the mints, they will not be successful in shade. They also require a deeply dug, well-drained soil. If this is not drained, work in some lime rubble such as mortar from old buildings, crushed brick, or shingle. Herbs require humus, but little manure and no artificial fertilisers. Some thoroughly decayed cow manure or peat mixed with used hops will be suitable, as will material from a compost heap or clearings from ditches.

Planting is best done in spring. Allow ample space between the plants, for many will grow tall and even the shortest will grow bushy. Most are perennial and will occupy the ground for many years, so remove all weeds before planting.

Cutting the plants from time to time as the leaves are required will usually prevent them from growing too large, but any unduly long shoots should be removed at the end of summer when the plants are made tidy for winter. They are then given a mulch of whatever materials are available—a mixture of sifted soil, peat and decayed manure being ideal.

In the first year there will be only a few leaves to cut, as the plants are building up and will need most of their foliage to survive their first winter, especially if one of severity. In the second year, they may be liberally cut which will encourage them to form more and more shoots from the base. Unduly long shoots are cut back to halfway and each plant should be prevented from growing into the next one by the removal of necessary growth.

The young leaves are the richest in fragrance and flavour. If any are to be dried for winter use, remove them towards the end of summer when at their best and quite dry. Spread them out on sheets of paper in an airy room, turning daily until they are crisp to the touch, or string them up in small bunches to dry. They should then be put through a sieve to remove the stalks and fibres and the leafy part put into bottles or wooden containers, labelled and placed in a dry room or cupboard to be used as required. Remember always to replace the cap firmly after use, otherwise the herbs will soon lose their strength. Plants such as angelica, grown for their stems, should be cut regularly so that they do not become tough. Seeds must be harvested when fully ripe and dry, but before the pods open and the seeds are scattered.

Tall-growing Plants
At the back plant fennel, a perennial with finely divided leaves which grows 3–4ft tall and bears its flowers in large umbels. It is a common plant of waste sandy places, especially close to the sea. Like the handsome Alexanders, its scented leaves and stems are much in demand to make sauces to serve with fish. They also give soups and stews a pleasant flavour. The seed was once used to flavour bread and cakes (like caraway) and the accounts of Edward I, for 1281, record that 8lb were bought by the royal household as one month's supply. Later, the seed was used to flavour gin, whilst fennel-water, obtained from the seed, is a valuable carminative.

Fennel grows best in a chalky soil which is normally well drained.

Seed is sown in drills in July and the young plants moved to the herb garden early in April. There is a bronzy-leaf variety which makes a striking plant for the herb garden or border.

Angelica is also perennial and grows to a similar height. *Angelica sylvestris*, our native form, has two to three pinnate leaves and bears umbels of white flowers from July onwards. It is found in damp woodlands and along the sides of woods. In past times it had so many valuable qualities that it was thought to be of heavenly origin. The dried roots, powdered, were taken to calm the nerves, whilst water made from the roots is an aid to digestive disorders. The seed is used to this day by the monks of La Grande Chartreuse to flavour their famous liqueur.

A more vigorous form *A archangelica*, native of Greenland, Iceland and Scandinavia, and for long grown in British gardens, is often found wild as a garden escapee, mostly in damp woodlands near villages. All parts of the plant are more strongly scented and it should be grown instead of *A sylvestris* as its properties are more reliable. When cut into small pieces and stewed with rhubarb (one stem to six stems of rhubarb), angelica stems impart a delicious musky flavour. When boiled in sugar, they turn brilliant green and, when candied, make a pleasant sweetmeat. Boil for five minutes, then peel the stems and boil again in the syrup until all the moisture has evaporated. Sprinkle with castor sugar, let the stems stand for two days, then boil for a few minutes more, until the sugar has dissolved, and place in a jar to use as required. Small pieces may be chopped and used on home-made biscuits and buns, or to flavour ice cream.

Though the angelica is perennial, the stems are more tender and the roots of more value if it is treated as biennial, sowing the seeds in the border where the plants are to mature, or, alternatively, it will seed itself if the soil is undisturbed. It is one of the few herbs to be tolerant of partial shade, so, if in full sun, provide it with plenty of moisture in summer. For the stems to be tender, it should be grown uickly.

Lovage, *Ligusticum scoticum*, is also a plant for the back of the border, growing 3ft tall with purple stems and glossy leaves which have the flavour of celery and may be chopped and used in salads or cooked with stews. The plant is believed to have come with the Romans for it grows in profusion around Liguria and it was also used for scenting baths. Dr Turner, a native of Northumberland, where the plant grows naturally (perhaps introduced there by Roman legions when building Hadrian's Wall), said that an infusion of the leaves in hot water would ease a sore throat if used for gargling. If they were crushed, fried in lard and then placed on a boil, he believed that the leaves would quickly bring it to a head.

Lovage is propagated by root division in spring, or from seed sown in July and transplanted to the herb garden in April.

Another umbellifer which has leaves of similar fragrance is *Apium graveolens*, the wild celery, from which the garden variety was evolved. A biennial, growing 2–3ft tall, it has toothed pinnate leaves and bears its white flowers in umbels during July and August. The leaves are used in soups and stews whilst a few, finely chopped, may be put in salads.

Chervil is a plant which has been long naturalised here. An annual, growing about 18in tall, it has three-pinnate leaves, pubescent on the underside and emitting the scent of aniseed when bruised. The plant takes its name, *Chaerophyllum*, from two Greek words meaning that which 'rejoices the heart' from the 'warming' qualities of the leaves which make a welcome addition to a salad. They may also be used to make a sauce to serve with fish. To maintain a supply, sow in August where it is to grow to maturity, and again in April and at monthly intervals until July.

Sweet chervil is not to be confused with sweet cicely, *Myrrhis odorata*, a pubescent perennial growing 3ft tall, its stem hollow and furrowed, and with fragrant pale-green pinnate leaves. Slow growing, sweet cicely may reach a height of 5–6ft and should be raised from seed sown where they are to grow and thinned to 2ft apart. The plants, as with all perennial umbellifers, will be longer living if not allowed to set seed. They tend to die back in winter but will make new growth again in spring. It is a plant, like anglica, of the cooler climate of the north and is rare south of Lincolnshire. It emits a myrrh-like smell when handled and though the fern-like leaves are hot and spicy, they taste, like those of chervil, as if they have been steeped in boiled sugar. They are used in salads and stews, whilst the roots may be boiled and served with a white sauce. They were also candied, like eringoes, to eat as sweets and the leaves boiled as a substitute for spinach.

The caraway is a biennial growing 2ft tall, with a parsnip-like root which also has a similar flavour. The two-pinnate leaves are cut into linear lobes, like those of parsley and may be used in a similar manner. The fruit (seed) is boat-shaped with small ridges, its name being derived from the Gaelic *caroh*, 'a ship'. It is a rare plant of waste ground, mostly in Essex and East Anglia where it will ripen its seed in a good summer, but rarely elsewhere.

The dried seeds will retain their scent for a long time and may be used in muslin sachets placed among clothes to which they will impart a camphor-like smell and keep away moths. From the seeds, a spiced wine, *Aqua compositis* was made, which Henry VIII found especially to his liking. Today, they are used to flavour the liqueur kümmel. Half an ounce of seed infused in a pint of boiling water and allowed to cool will, if taken in small doses, relieve flatulence. In Ireland, the seed is added to home-made bread and cakes, but the flavour is not to everyone's taste.

Herbs of Compact Habit

Salad burnet, *Poterium sanguisorba*, is of the rose family, a neat perennial growing 15in tall. It has finely toothed pinnate leaves which, when pressed, release the mossy smell of cucumbers. The tiny flowers, borne from May until September in a capitate cyme, are green, tinted with purple. The calyx tube is four-winged. Common in downland country in southern England (especially in Wiltshire), north-east Yorkshire, and also western Ireland, it continues to grow through winter.

Salad burnet was planted in Tudor gardens, with chamomile and creeping thyme. Parkinson and Culpeper said that the leaves were used in salads and in sandwiches with cheese, also to flavour cider, imparting a pleasant 'quick' taste, possibly reinforcing Pliny's opinion that it obtained its name from the Greek *poterion*, 'a drinking cup'. Seed is sown in early summer, the young plants being set out 10in apart in autumn. The first leaves will be ready to remove towards the end of the following summer, taking several from each plant so as not to cause excessive defoliation until they are well established. To prolong the life of the plants, remove the flowers as they form.

For an edging to a garden of native herbs, chives may be planted 6–8in apart. Widespread across northern Europe and Asia, from

Britain to the wastes of Siberia, this plant is often found on cliffs near the sea and around the sides of lakes. It grows 6–8in high, with cylindrical rush-like leaves which are evergreen. A member of the onion family, the chive, *Allium schoenoprasum*, is mild of flavour and readily digestible. It may be cut near the base and chopped into soups and stews; or used in sandwiches with cream cheese or hard-boiled eggs, with omelettes, or sprinkled on a Welsh rarebit. They also add interest to a salad.

In past times, the plants, which form a tuft of rush-like stems, were grown in pots on kitchen window-ledges and were known as seives. Propagation is by lifting and dividing the plants in late autumn, pulling the offsets apart and replanting into soil containing some humus, preferably in the form of decayed manure or used hops.

Quite as useful in the kitchen is parsley, *Petroselinum crispum*, found on old walls as a garden escapee and on rocks near the sea, hence its botanical name which literally means 'growing on rocks'. Parsley is the richest source of vitamin A of all vegetables; it is also rich in vitamins C and E and in iron salts. The emerald-green leaves, crisped and curled, make an admirable edging. Growing 9in tall, the plants may be grown in pots or a window box to provide 'green' all the year to use for garnishing, to make sauce to enjoy with fish (especially halibut), and to sprinkle over soups and stews, egg dishes and salads. Parsley will freeze well after blanching in boiling water for two minutes. Fresh seed only must be sown, otherwise it will not germinate. Sow in April in rows 10in apart. Parsley requires a deeply worked soil containing plenty of humus so that the plants will run to seed in hot, dry weather.

The common chamomile, *Anthemis nobilis*, is an almost prostrate perennial with a much-branched stem, forming a dense mat. The leaves are cut into segments and, when walked upon, emit an aromatic fruity scent. Because of this, the Spanish call it *manzinella*, 'little apple'. The plant was used in Tudor times to make a scented 'lawn'. For this purpose, plants are raised from seed sown in drills in April. In autumn, when the 'lawn' is made, plant the chamomile 6in apart into soil which has been rolled flat. The ground must be kept weeded the first year until the plants spread out to suppress all annual weeds and form a thick evergreen mat which remains green during the hottest weather. Towards the end of summer, clip hard back and roll the plants when dry. John Evelyn said 'it will now [October] be good to beat, roll and mow the carpet walks of chamomile'.

To make a 'tea' to soothe tired nerves, use 1 oz of the fresh flowers to a pint of boiling water. The same preparation is valuable as a hair tonic to massage into the scalp. The daisy-like flowers should be removed when just open for then their medicinal value will be at its greatest.

Parkinson compared the pungency of the leaves to those of featherfew, and, before the introducton of tobacco, the leaves of both these plants were dried and smoked whilst the more finely ground leaves were taken as snuff.

Featherfew is *Chrysanthemum parthenium*, a branched perennial readily raised from seed, which grows about 15in tall, the one to two narrow leaflets being divided into lobed segments. The dried leaves, placed in muslin bags and amongst clothes will help to keep away moths, and will give immediate relief if applied fresh to insect bites. Culpeper said that a decoction of the fresh leaves with a little honey would help to ease a hard cough. Seed is sown in a frame in March, or outdoors in drills in April, and the plants set out when large enough to handle. Plant them 12in apart.

The wormwood, *Artemesia absinthium*, of the same family, grows to a similar height and is in bloom during July and August, with tiny yellow buttons appearing in small heads. The leaves, which are divided into blunt segments or lobes, are covered on both sides in thick down and are powerfully aromatic.

Common on waste ground throughout Britain, the plant was used in medieval times to strew over earthen floors to keep away insects, and Gerard said it would keep the air cool in summer. The dried leaves may be mixed with those of featherfew, to place amongst clothes. Tusser was correct in recommending wormwood 'tea' sweetened with honey as a general tonic, for the plant is rich in nitrate of potash which acts as a stimulant. It is used in the manufacture of absinth. Plant in spring 18in apart as it grows to about that height, and the same across.

The closely related *A vulgaris*, the mugwort, grows 2–3ft tall and has dark green leaves which are covered with down on the underside. The yellowish-brown flowers, like those of mimosa, are borne in short spikes from July until September. It takes its name from the

20 Tansy

Saxon *moughte*, 'a moth', for the dried leaves will keep moths from clothes, whilst a sprig, carried in the buttonhole, will keep away flies in warm, thundery weather. Before hops were used to clarify ale, mugwort leaves were in demand for the same purpose.

A nourishing beer is made from the plant, using 3oz of the leaves to every 2gal of water. Simmer for an hour, add 1lb of brown sugar and place in an earthenware pan. Add a tablespoonful of yeast and allow to ferment for ten to twelve days; then strain into bottles and cork when fermentation has finished.

Plant offsets in spring 18in apart or raise plants from seed sown in drills in April, moving to their permanent places when large enough to handle.

Tansy, *Tanacetum vulgare*, grows to a similar height, its dark green pinnate leaves being deeply toothed, its flowers, like yellow buttons, being borne in generous clusters from July until late autumn. It takes its name from the Greek *athanasia*, 'immortality', because it remains so long in bloom. The camphor-smelling leaves keep away flies and also fleas, so for this reason were placed amongst bedding. They were also rubbed onto meat to hide any unpleasant taste or smell should the meat not be completely fresh. If soaked in milk or buttermilk for ten days, it makes a soothing complexion milk.

It is a striking plant in the garden and is propagated by lifting and replanting pieces of the rootstock 2ft apart, in autumn; or from seed sown in April, moving the young plants to the herb garden in July. The variety *foliis crispis* is the more attractive form, its almost fern-like leaves being brilliant emerald-green and highly scented.

The Pungent Labiates

A number of the labiates grow in Britain and are valuable plants for a herb garden, though most are native of the Mediterranean regions. They are found mostly in calcareous soils and require an open sunny situation to be at their best. The white horehound, *Marrubium vulgare*, is widespread on downland and by the wayside. It is perennial and grows 20in tall, its square stems being covered in down whilst the white flowers are borne in dense whorls. They are much visited by bees in the late summer months.

The plant takes its name from the Hebrew *marrob*, 'bitter juice'. A familiar plant of the Near East, it was one of the five bitter herbs which the Jews were ordered to take during the Passover. Since earliest times, syrup of horehound mixed with honey was taken for a hard cough, whilst a delicious tonic beer was brewed from the leaves.

Horehound 'tea' is an excellent tonic. To 1oz of the fresh leaves add 1pt of boiling water; sweeten with a little honey, then strain and drink a wineglassful daily.

The plant is evergreen in all but the hardest of winters. To propagate, lift and divide in March or raise plants from seed sown in April. A well-drained soil is necessary for the plants to be long lived.

Marjoram, *Origanum vulgare*, grows about 12in tall, its short-stalked leaves being covered in down whilst its rosy-purple flowers are borne in terminal cymes late in summer. It is present on hilly pastures throughout England and Wales but rare in Scotland. Marjoram has a stimulating scent and in hot, dry weather secretes an essential oil with a camphor-like smell from the stems and leaves. If the fresh leaves are placed in a warm bath, they will relieve nervous tension and a 'tea' made from an infusion of the leaves in boiling water, and taken cold before bedtime, will encourage sound sleep. The dried leaves are used in stuffings and to sprinkle over soups.

Plants are readily raised from seed sown in a frame or under cloches in spring, the young plants being moved to the herb garden early in summer. Plant 10in apart in a well-drained soil.

Balm, native to southern Europe may have come with the Romans, for it has long been naturalised in Britain where it is present on downland slopes, mostly in the south of England. It is perennial, growing 2ft tall with deeply wrinkled pale green leaves and with white flowers borne in whorls from the leaf joints. The leaves release a delicious lemony scent when bruised and were used to impart their 'sharp' refreshing flavour to drinks. 1oz of the leaves to a pint of boiling water makes a refreshing tonic drink. Add the juice of half a lemon and sweeten with a little honey. The young leaves, finely chopped and used sparingly, make a pleasant addition to a salad; or use them with cheese in sandwiches.

Balm, *Melissa officinalis*, makes a bushy plant as wide as it is tall and requires a humus-laden soil to grow well. It is best propagated from cuttings taken in July and rooted in a frame or in boxes of sandy soil. Plant out 2ft apart. The plant takes its name from the Latin *melissi*, 'honey', from the large secretion of nectar by the flowers which are much frequented by bees. There is a form with attractive golden leaf markings which adds interest to the herb garden.

Wild thyme, *Thymus drucei*, is a perennial under-shrub with short-stalked leaves covered in glandular dots which are aromatic when pressed. It is present throughout Britain on dry banks and sand dunes, the reddish-purple flowers appearing throughout summer. They are eagerly worked by bees. During medieval times, when honey was the only form of sweetening, beds of thyme were greatly prized. The leaves were used to stuff the richer meats.

Thyme is propagated either from seed sown in April or by taking cuttings in July. If taken with a heel they will soon root in a sandy compost. Plant 12in apart to the front of the herb garden.

The mints should be in every garden and may be grown in a shady corner where little else will flourish. They are not particularly attractive in appearance, but have so many uses as to be almost indispensable. Peppermint, *Mentha piperita*, grows 12in tall and is often found by the wayside in parts of Lincolnshire and Cambridgeshire where it was at one time grown commercially for the extraction of its oil, so much in demand to flavour confectionery. As with lavender, English oil of peppermint has a purity exceeding all others. One drop on a handkerchief for inhaling will relieve a head cold and taken on a lump of sugar will relieve flatulence or a feeling of sickness.

Apple mint, *M rotundifolia*, grows twice as tall, the small oval leaves having the smell of ripe apples, whilst it makes a delicious mint sauce to serve with lamb and green peas. It is distinguished from other mints by its pale green stem and leaves.

Spearmint, *M spicata*, grows 12in tall and has lanceolate leaves of brilliant green which, when pressed, release a powerful peppermint smell. When used with *M rotundifolia* it makes the best mint sauce. To make mint vinegar, fill a glass jar with the fresh leaves of the apple mint and spearmint and pour over them a quart of malt vinegar. Allow to stand for three weeks before bottling.

Mints should be planted in November, dividing the creeping rootstock into small pieces and planting 2in deep. Some decayed manure should have been incorporated into the soil. Calamint, *Calamintha ascendens*, requires a dry soil and is found on sunny banks and mountainous slopes. It has a creeping rootstock and grows 9in high. It is a plant of shrubby habit like the thymes and may be planted between paving stones. An infusion of the leaves in hot water is an excellent remedy for flatulence and indigestion.

Wild basil, *C vulgaris*, grows to about the same height and is a downy perennial with pointed oval leaves and bearing whorls of mauve-pink flowers through late summer and autumn. It is found on dry banks and by the wayside throughout much of England and in the garden requires similar conditions to the calamint. Though the leaves are not so pungently scented it is an interesting little plant and worthy of a place in the wild-flower garden.

11

PROPAGATING WILD FLOWERS

There is a vital spirit in every seed to beget its like.

Nicholas Culpeper, *The Complete Herbal*

Although one should never uproot wild flowers to plant in the garden, there is no harm in removing the seed when their flowering season has ended and they are ripe for sowing in boxes at home. If the seed capsules are removed with care, without in any way loosening the plant, this will prolong the life of many perennials which will not have to use their energy in the production of too much seed, whilst annual and biennial plants will, in any case, die after flowering.

The months of flowering of all the wild flowers mentioned here as being suitable for garden culture, are given in Appendix B. The plants can be expected to have ripened their seed about two months after they have finished flowering. Much will depend upon the weather during summer and autumn as dry, sunny days are needed for the plants to ripen their seeds before mid-October when the winter rains can be expected and by which time ripening will have ended. The spring-flowering plants, however, will have ripened their seed by midsummer from when they should be looked over with care so that the capsules can be removed just on the point of opening and before the seeds are spilled. Do not remove every capsule from a given plant, take one here and there, so that the others will fall to the ground and germinate, thus ensuring the constant reproduction of the species.

Saving Seed

When removing the capsules, preferably on a dry day, do so with a pair of pointed scissors, cutting away the whole stalk so as not to pull or loosen the plant. After their removal (and seeds may also be saved in this way from wild flowers growing in the garden) place the capsules in small muslin or paper bags with the stems protruding and tie securely so that the seeds will not be lost. Insert a slip of paper with the name of the species and date collected into each bag. Many seeds will be available by the wayside but, if entering woodlands or fields, remember to do so with the utmost care for the property, closing any gates.

The seed capsules should finish drying in an airy room. An attic is ideal, or a garden room or shed. The contents of the bags are spread out on sheets of clean brown paper, together with the name slips. Keep each species separate so that it may be given the cultural conditions it best enjoys when planting in the garden.

As the capsules dry, which will take a week to ten days, squeeze out the seeds carefully, as some will be as small as dust and may easily be lost. Place them in matchboxes, clearly named, for sowing at the required time. Seed of the spring-flowering plants is best sown as soon as harvested, possibly early in July, for the seedlings will then be established before winter, sowing them in boxes in a frame or in a cold greenhouse and moving them to the open ground when large enough to handle. Biennials, those plants which will bloom the following year, will also be sown in July, but seed of annuals should be kept until the following year, sowing in a frame or greenhouse early in the New Year, or in April in the open ground where the plants are to bloom.

Sowing the Seed

If sowing in boxes, use a John Innes sowing compost. This is sterilised and no weeds nor disease spores will be introduced to compete with the wild-flower seeds, often bringing about their destruction in the seedling stage. The J I compost, obtainable from most garden shops and nurserymen, is made up of

2 parts	sterilised loam	
1 part	peat	
1 part	coarse sand	per bushel
1¾ oz	superphosphate of lime	
¼ oz	ground chalk	

This formula is suitable for almost all wild flowers. The compost should be obtained freshly made, for superphosphate soon loses its strength and it is necessary to encourage the young plants to form a vigorous rooting system.

Boxes or pans are filled with compost to within ½in of the top, to allow for watering. The compost should be in a friable condition and, before sowing, the surface made quite level so that the seeds will have the same covering of compost throughout. Sow thinly, scattering the seed evenly over the surface and cover with compost as lightly as possible. Water carefully, preferably immersing the base of the container in a sink containing clean water, and cover with a sheet of clean glass or polythene to encourage rapid germination. Do not forget to note the name of the seeds and date of sowing.

Never allow the compost to dry out otherwise germination will be delayed. Water only when necessary, however, as too wet a compost may cause the seeds to decay. Keep it comfortably moist. When the seedlings have formed their second pair of leaves—that is, when large enough to handle—transplant them to boxes containing fresh compost and plant them 1in apart. Use a small piece of stick or cane, made smooth at one end, to loosen the young seedling. Then, holding the plant between the fingers of one hand, transfer it to the second box where a hole is made in the compost with the dibber to take the roots. Firm in with the back of the hand, then make the next transplant. The plants should be grown on for several weeks, either in a frame or in the open, until ready to be moved to their flowering quarters.

Plants such as cowslips and primroses may be given their first move to open-ground beds, rather than to boxes, where they are planted 1in apart in soil that has been fortified by a little peat and decayed manure. The plants must be kept moist by regular watering in dry weather, which is best done in the evening, giving the ground a soaking whenever necessary.

Poppies, pansies and most annuals and biennials, are best raised by sowing the seed directly into drills outdoors and later transplanting the seedlings to their flowering quarters. For those plants not amenable to transplanting sow directly into the ground where they are to bloom. Sow thinly, scattering the seed in circles and raking into the surface. If sowing in drills, make the drills with the back of a rake, no

H

more than 1in deep. At all times keep the soil moist to encourage germination and do not forget to name the rows (or circles) either on a plan or with markers.

For those unable to collect their own seeds from wild flowers, a large number of species are obtainable from specialist seedsmen such as Messrs Thompson & Morgan of Ipswich. Unlike many hybrid plants, seed saved from the wild-flower species will come true from seed, whilst fresh seed is most reliable as to germination. Seed that is more than a year old may not germinate at all, and so prove a disappointment.

Propagation By Division

Most wild flowers of perennial habit may also be increased by division of the roots—cowslips and primroses, in particular, lending themselves to this form of propagation as well as any other plants forming tufts or rosettes of leaves. It will be advisable to lift the clumps every four or five years when they will have formed numerous offsets, each of which can be detached and replanted to form another clump in two or three years' time.

After flowering has ended, the early autumn is a suitable time to divide many perennials. Lift the plants with a small border fork and shake off most of the soil. Then hold the plants firmly in both hands and gently 'tease' apart the numerous offsets. Each piece will come away with some roots, and a single plant will often produce a dozen or more plants to re-set at the required distance apart. At this time, it will be advisable to work some leaf mould and a little decayed manure into the ground and this should be repeated whenever the plants are lifted and divided. In this way the vigour of the plants will be maintained. If one or two clumps are divided each year there will be no falling off in the display, for the older plants will continue to be a mass of bloom, whilst the newly planted offsets are re-establishing themselves.

Many plants may also be divided in the spring but, for those which bloom at this time, autumn planting will enable them to re-establish themselves before the frosts. In this way they will give a limited display of bloom the following year.

Planting Bulbs

Most bulbs are planted in late autumn to bloom during spring and early summer. The one or two exceptions such as the autumn-flowering crocus and meadow saffron are planted in spring or early summer.

Bulbs of the *Amaryllidacea* family, snowdrops and snowflakes, may be moved whilst still 'green', immediately after flowering, and will then bloom the following year. They are lifted with a garden fork, taking care to dig well under the clumps so as not to break away the leaves or damage the bulbs. Carefully shake away the soil, then break up the cluster of bulbs in the same way as when dividing an established border plant. Several bulbs should be removed together and the clusters replanted 12in apart as soon as possible, and before the bulbs can dry out. Plant them 3–4in deep with the foliage above ground. Always allow the foliage of bulbs to die back completely before removing it. This will not be necessary for those bulbs grow-in the wild garden where their dying foliage will be hidden by long grass.

Where obtaining snowdrops and snowflakes from specialist growers, it is better to do so whilst the plants are still 'green', and the grower will advise as to the correct time to move them. They should be planted as soon as received.

Those plants growing from a rhizome, such as Solomon's seal and the flag iris, are planted in autumn. The rhizomes are planted just beneath the soil surface and made firm. The iris should have a leaf bud clearly visible from which a tuft of sword-like leaves will appear in spring. To propagate the iris, the large rhizomatous root is lifted in autumn when all flowering has ended and the rhizomes detached with a sharp knife, each piece or section having a leaf which will form the plant, and which will die back in winter. Fibrous roots will be seen growing from the woody rootstock.

Lily-of-the-valley is grown from crowns, rather like peonies, which should be planted in November for only at this time are the roots dormant. With peonies, care must be taken that the 'eyes', which are the foliage and flowerbuds, do not become detached from the roots and, as they are brittle, they must be handled with care They should be planted with the 'eyes' only just beneath soil level.

With many bulbs, upon lifting, there will be found growing around the larger bulbs or corms numbers of tiny bulblets (or cormlets) which may be detached and grown on to a larger size for planting out in two years' time. They are planted in boxes or frames containing a friable compost, spacing them 1in apart. Just cover with compost and keep comfortably moist. They will produce their foliage in spring and summer to die back in the normal way when watering is discontinued in autumn. They should be started into growth again the following spring and will be ready to plant out in autumn. Some will bloom in the spring of the next year, but others may take another year before they do so.

Most bulbs are readily raised from seed but some will take several years to come into bloom. The flowering garlics, bluebells and lily-of-the-valley can usually be brought into bloom within three years of sowing seed, but snowdrops, snowflakes, tulips and narcissi will take at least four years.

Other Methods of Propagation

Amongst the easiest of plants to propagate are those like the periwinkle and ground ivy which have trailing stems and form roots at the leaf joints. They will take root when in contact with the soil and may then be severed from the parent plant by cutting the stem with scissors and lifting the part which has rooted. It may then be replanted in a pot to grow on or planted directly into the open ground. Both these plants, which retain their leaves all year, may be used in hanging baskets and window boxes where they will make a most attractive display.

Pinks are propagated from seed or by 'slips'. These are unflowered shoots which are detached by pulling them from the main stem. They will come away with a 'heel' or piece of stem attached and from here the roots will quickly form if the 'slips' are inserted in boxes of sand and peat and kept moist. They may also be propagated from 'pipings' —the upper portion of a cutting or shoot which has not flowered— which is removed by holding it with finger and thumb above a leaf joint and gently pulling in an upwards direction, when it will come cleanly away. These are inserted around the sides of an earthenware pot, containing a sand and peat compost, to root. They are then transferred to small individual pots in which they remain through winter, to be planted out the following spring.

Hard-wooded plants such as heaths and *hypericums*—indeed all plants of shrubby habit—may be propagated by removing the shoots (preferably unflowered) with a sharp knife when they are about 3in long. These are known as cuttings. The base is inserted in hormone powder, to encourage rapid rooting, before placing in a compost of sand and peat, either in boxes or around the sides of a pot. They will be ready for planting out in about twelve months but, after rooting, it is preferable to move them to small pots to grow on for several months. They can then be planted out with their root ball intact and will grow without check. After treating the cuttings with hormone, plant them 1in apart and make them quite firm in the compost.

APPENDIX A

WILD FLOWERS AND THEIR COMMON NAMES

Species	Common Name
Achillea millefolium	yarrow
Achillea ptarmica	sneezewort
Acorus calamus	sweet flag
Agrimonia eupatoria	common agrimony
Agrostemma githago	corn cockle
Althaea palustris	marsh mallow
Alyssum maritimum	sweet alyssum
Anagallis arvensis	scarlet pimpernel
Anchusa officinalis	alkanet
Anemone nemorosa	wood anemone
Antirrhinum majus	snapdragon
Aquilegia vulgaris	columbine
Arabis caucasica	arabis
Arbutus unedo	strawberry tree
Armeria maritima	thrift
Bellis perennis	daisy
Berberis vulgaris	barberry
Borago officinalis	borage
Butomus umbellatus	flowering rush
Calamintha ascendens	calamint
Calluna vulgaris	ling
Caltha palustris	marsh marigold
Campanula latifolia	giant bellflower; rocket
Campanula medium	Canterbury bell
Campanula rapunculus	rampion
Campanula rotundifolia	harebell; bluebell of Scotland
Cardamine pratensis	lady's smock; cuckoo flower
Centaurea cyanus	cornflower
Cerastium cerastoides	starwort mouse-ear
Cheiranthus cheiri	wallflower
Chrysanthemum leucanthemum	ox-eye daisy; moon penny; marguerite
Chrysosplenium oppositifolium	golden saxifrage
Colchicum autumnale	meadow saffron
Convallaria majalis	lily-of-the-valley; wood lily
Cotoneaster microphyllus	rockspray
Cotyledon umbilicus	navelwort
Crataegus monogyna	hawthorn; may
Crocus nudiflorus	autumn crocus; naked lady
Cyclamen europeum	common cyclamen

Species	Common Name
Cynoglossum officinale	hound's tongue
Cytisus scoparius	broom
Daphne laureola	spurge laurel
Daphne mezereum	mezereon
Delphinium consolida	larkspur; lark's-heels
Dianthus gratianopolitanus	Cheddar pink
Dianthus caryophyllus	common pink
Dianthus deltoides	maiden pink
Diapensia lapponica	diapensia
Digitalis purpurea	foxglove
Diplotaxis tenuifolia	wall rocket
Drosera rotundifolia	common sundew
Dryas octopetala	mountain avens
Echium vulgare	viper's bugloss
Endymion nonscriptus	bluebell; wild hyacinth
Epilobium angustifolium	rosebay; willowherb
Epilobium hirsutum	great willowherb
Epipactis helleborine	common helleborine
Eranthis hyemalis	winter aconite
Erica ciliaris	Dorset heath
Erica hibernica	Irish heath
Erica vagans	Cornish heather
Erica vulgaris	ling; heather
Eryngium maritimum	sea holly
Eupatorium cannabinum	hemp agrimony
Euphorbia amygdaloides	wood spurge
Fritillaria meleagris	chequered daffodil; ginny-hen flower
Fumaria officinalis	fumitory
Gagea lutea	yellow star of Bethlehem
Galanthus nivalis	snowdrop; Candlemas bells
Gentiana verna	spring gentian
Geranium phaeum	dusky cranesbill
Geranium pratense	meadow cranesbill
Geranium robertianum	herb Robert
Geranium sanguineum	bloody cranesbill
Geum rivale	water avens
Geum urbanum	herb bennet; blessed herb; wood avens
Glechoma hederacea	ground ivy; ale-hoof
Helianthemum apenninum	white rock-rose
Helianthemum chamaecistus	common rock-rose
Helleborus foetidus	stinking hellebor
Helleborus niger	Christmas rose
Helleborus viridis	green helleborine
Hesperis matronalis	dame's violet; sweet rocket
Hottonia palustris	water violet
Hypericum androsaemum	tutsan; all-heal
Hypericum calycinum	rose of Sharon
Hypericum hirsutum	hairy St John's wort
Hypericum humifusum	trailing St John's wort

Species	Common Name
Hypericum perforatum	common St John's wort
Iberis amara	wild candy tuft
Impatiens biflora	orange balsam
Impatiens glandulifera	water or Himalayan balsam
Impatiens noli-tangere	touch-me-not
Inula helenium	elecampane
Iris foetidissima	roast-beef plant; gladdon
Iris pseudacorus	yellow flag
Leonurus cardiaca	motherwort
Leucojum aestivum	summer snowflake
Leucojum vernum	spring snowflake
Ligustrum vulgare	privet
Limonium binervosum	rock sea lavender
Limonium vulgare	sea lavender
Lonicera caprifolium	perfoliate honeysuckle
Lonicera periclymenum	woodbine; honeysuckle
Lupinus arboreus	tree lupin
Lycopsis arvensis	small bugloss
Lymnanthemum nymphaeoides	fringed water-lily
Lysimachia nummularia	creeping jenny
Lysimachia vulgaris	yellow loosestrife
Lythrum salicaria	purple loosestrife
Mahonia aquifolium	Oregon grape
Malus sylvestris	crab apple
Malva sylvestris	mallow
Matthiola incana	hoary stock
Matthiola sinuata	great sea stock
Mentha aquatica	water mint
Mentha pulegium	pennyroyal
Mentha rotundifolia	apple mint
Mentha sylvestris	woodland mint
Mimulus guttatus	monkey flower
Muscari racemosum	grape hyacinth
Myosotis alpestris	alpine forget-me-not
Myosotis arvensis	forget-me-not; mouse-ear
Myosotis sylvatica	wood forget-me-not
Myrica gale	bog myrtle
Narcissus poeticus	poet's narcissus
Narcissus pseudonarcissus	wild daffodill; Lent lily
Nepeta cataria	catmint
Nuphar lutea	yellow water-lily
Nymphaea alba	white water-lily
Oenanthe fistulosa	water dropwort
Oenothera biennis	evening primrose
Orchis morio	green-winged orchid
Origanum marjorana	marjoram
Ornithogalum nutans	nodding star of Bethlehem
Ornithogalum umbellatum	star of Bethlehem
Oxalis floribunda	pink oxalis

Species	Common Name
Paeonia corallina	peony
Papaver rhoeas	corn poppy
Papaver somniferum	opium poppy
Paris quadrifolia	herb Paris
Peucedanum ostruthium	pink masterwort
Polemonium coeruleum	Jacob's ladder
Polygonatum multiflorum	Solomon's seal
Polygonum bistorta	bistort
Potentilla erecta	yellow cinquefoil
Potentilla palustris	March cinquefoil
Primula farinosa	oxlip
Primula farinosa	birdseye primrose
Primula veris	cowslip; paigle
Primula vulgaris	primrose
Prunus padus	bird cherry
Pulmonaria officinalis	lungwort; soldiers and sailors
Pulsatilla vulgaris	Easter flower; Pasque flower
Pyrola minor	wintergreen
Pyrola uniflora	St Olaf's candlestick
Pyrus cerasifera	cherry-plum
Ranunculus lingua	greater spearwort
Ranunculus ficaria	lesser celandine
Rosa arvensis	field rose; musk rose
Rosa canina	dog rose; wild rose
Rosa rubiginosa	sweetbriar; eglantine
Sagina nodosa	knotted pearlwort
Sagina procumbens	mossy pearlwort
Sagina saginoides	alpine pearlwort
Sagittaria sagitifolia	arrowhead
Salvia horminoides	clary; clear eyes
Salvia pratensis	meadow sage
Sambucus nigra	elder
Saponaria officinalis	soapwort
Saussurea alpina	purple hawkweed
Saxifraga aizoides	mountain saxifrage
Saxifraga hypnoides	mossy saxifrage
Saxifraga oppositifolia	purple saxifrage
Saxifraga stellaris	starry saxifrage
Saxifraga umbrosa	London pride
Scabiosa arvensis	field scabious
Scilla verna	spring squill
Scirpus lacustris	bullrush
Scirpus maritimus	sea club-rush
Scirpus palustris	common spike-rush
Scrophularia aquatica	water figwort
Sedum acre	stonecrop
Sedum album	white stonecrop
Sedum anglicum	English stonecrop
Sedum roseum	rose-root
Sedum rupestre	rock stonecrop
Silene acaulis	moss campion
Smyrnium olusatrum	Alexanders

Species	Common Name
Sorbus aria	white beam
Sorbus aucuparia	rowan; mountain ash
Sorbus torminalis	wild service
Spiraea ulmaria	meadowsweet
Stachys betonica	lamb's ear, wood betony
Tamarix anglica	tamarisk
Teucrium chamaedrys	wall germander
Teucrium scordium	water germander
Teucrium scorodonia	wood sage
Thlaspi alpestre	alpine pennycress
Thymus drucei	wild thyme
Thymus serpyllum	mountain thyme
Trollius europeus	globe flower
Tulipa sylvestris	wood tulip
Typha latifolia	false bullrush
Ulex europeus	gorse; whin
Valeriana officinalis	valerian; all-heal
Verbascum lychnitis	white mullein
Verbascum nigrum	black mullein
Verbascum thapsus	mullein
Verbena officinalis	vervain; verbena
Veronica alpina	alpine speedwell
Veronica tenella	mountain speedwell
Viburnum lantana	wayfaring tree
Viburnum opulus	guelder rose
Vinca minor	lesser periwinkle
Viola lutea	mountain pansy
Viola odorata	violet
Viola tricolor	pansy; heartsease; love-in-idleness; Pinkney John

APPENDIX B

THE WILD-FLOWER CALENDAR

(The species will be in bloom during each month as indicated)

	Height	Colour
JANUARY		
Eranthis hyemalis	3in	yellow
Helleborus niger	10in	white
Vinca minor	9in	blue
FEBRUARY		
Daphne mezereum	2ft	reddish-purple
Eranthis hyemalis	3in	yellow
Galanthus nivalis	4in	white and green
Helleborus niger	10in	white
Helleborus viridis	10in	green
Leucojum vernum	6in	white and green
Ulex europeus	8ft	yellow
Vinca minor	9in	blue
MARCH		
Anemone nemorosa	6in	white
Bellis perennis	3in	white, pink
Caltha palustris	20in	yellow
Daphne mezereum	2ft	reddish-purple
Eranthis hyemalis	3in	yellow
Euphorbia amygdaloides	15in	dull yellow
Galanthus nivalis	4in	white and green
Helleborus foetidus	3ft	greenish-yellow
Helleborus niger	10in	white
Helleborus viridis	10in	green
Leucojum vernum	6in	white and green
Mahonia aquifolium	3ft	yellow
Myosotis arvensis	6in	blue
Myosotis sylvatica	8in	pale blue
Myrica gale	3ft	catkins
Narcissus pseudonarcissus	12in	yellow
Primula vulgaris	4in	yellow
Prunus cerasifera	12ft	white
Prunus spinosa	10ft	white
Ranunculus ficaria	4in	yellow
Ulex europeus	8ft	yellow
Vinca minor	9in	blue
Viola canina	4in	purple-blue

135

	Height	*Colour*
APRIL		
Anemone nemorosa	6in	white
Arabis caucasica	4–6in	white
Bellis perennis	3in	white, pink
Caltha palustris	20in	yellow
Cheiranthus cheiri	15in	orange-yellow
Chrysosplenium oppositifolium	3in	yellow
Daphne laureola	2ft	green
Erica hibernica	4–5ft	mauve
Euphorbia amygdaloides	15in	dull yellow
Fritillaria meleagris	6in	chequered
Gagea lutea	5in	yellow
Gentiana verna	2in	blue
Glechoma hederacea	3in	purple
Helleborus foetidus	3ft	greenish-yellow
Helleborus niger	10in	white
Helleborus viridis	10in	green
Leucojum vernum	6in	white and green
Mahonia aquifolium	3ft	yellow
Muscari racemosum	6in	purple
Myosotis arvensis	6in	blue
Myosotis sylvatica	8in	pale blue
Myrica gale	3ft	catkins
Narcissus poeticus	15in	white
Narcissus pseudonarcissus	12in	yellow
Ornithogalum nutans	15in	green and white
Primula elatior	8in	buff
Primula veris	6in	yellow
Primula vulgaris	4in	yellow
Prunus cerasifera	12ft	white
Prunus spinosa	10ft	white
Pulmonaria officinalis	10in	pink and blue
Ranunculus ficaria	4in	yellow
Saxifraga oppositifolia	2in	purple
Scilla verna	4in	blue
Thlaspi alpestre	4–6in	white
Tulipa sylvestris	15in	yellow
Ulex europeus	8ft	yellow
Vinca minor	9in	blue
Viola canina	4in	purple-blue
Viola lutea	3in	yellow
Viola odorata	3in	purple
Viola tricolor	3in	yellow and blue
MAY		
Anchusa officinalis	3ft	blue
Anemone nemorosa	6in	white
Aquilegia vulgaris	2ft	navy-blue
Arabis caucasica	4–6in	white
Bellis perennis	3in	white, pink
Berberis vulgaris	2–3ft	lemon
Caltha palustris	20in	yellow
Cardamine pratense	18in	silver-blue
Cheiranthus cheiri	15in	orange-yellow

	Height	Colour
Chrysanthemum leucanthemum	15in	white
Convallaria majalis	8in	white
Cotoneaster microphyllus	6in	white
Crataegus monogyna	10ft	white
Crataegus oxyacanthoides	8ft	cream
Cytisus scoparius	8ft	yellow
Diapensia lapponica	3in	white
Diplotaxis tenuifolia	18in	yellow
Dryas octopetala	4in	white
Erica hibernica	4–5ft	mauve
Fritillaria meleagris	6in	chequered
Fumaria officinalis	1–2ft	pinkish-purple
Gagea lutea	5in	yellow
Gentiana verna	2in	blue
Geranium phaeum	18in	maroon
Geranium robertianum	9–12in	pink
Geum rivale	12in	orange-pink
Glechoma hederacea	3in	purple
Helianthemum appeninum	8in	white
Helianthemum chamaecistus	8in	yellow
Helleborus viridis	10in	green
Hottonia palustris	below surface	pale pink
Iris pseudacorus	3ft	yellow
Leucojum aestivum	9in	white
Lycopsis arvensis	9–10in	blue
Malus sylvestris	10ft	white and pink
Matthiola incana	10–12in	purple
Menyanthes trifoliata	surface	pink and white
Muscari racemosum	6in	purple
Myosotis arvensis	6in	blue
Myosotis sylvatica	8in	pale blue
Narcissus poeticus	15in	white
Orchis morio	9in	purple
Ornithogalum nutans	15in	green and white
Ornithogalum umbellatum	12in	white
Oxalis floribunda	8in	pink
Paeonia corallina	2ft	crimson
Paris quadrifolia	12in	green
Polygonatum multiflorum	2ft	white
Potentilla palustris	15in	maroon
Primula elatior	8in	buff
Primula farinosa	4in	pink
Primula veris	6in	yellow
Primula vulgaris	4in	yellow
Prunus padus	10ft	white
Pulmonaria officinalis	10in	pink and blue
Ranunculus ficaria	4in	yellow
Rosa spinosissima	3ft	cream
Saxifraga hypnoides	4–6in	pinkish-white
Saxifraga oppositifolia	2in	purple
Saxifraga umbrosa	8in	pink
Scilla verna	4in	blue
Scirpus palustris	18in	brown
Sedum roseum	8in	greenish

	Height	Colour
Smyrnium olusatrum	3–4ft	yellow
Sorbus aria	20ft	cream
Sorbus aucuparia	20ft	cream
Sorbus torminalis	20ft	cream
Thlaspi alpestre	4–6in	white
Thymus drucei	2in	purple
Tulipa sylvestris	15in	yellow
Ulex europeus	8ft	yellow
Viburnum lantana	10ft	creamy-white
Vinca minor	9in	blue
Viola canina	4in	purple-blue
Viola lutea	3in	yellow
Viola odorata	3in	purple
Viola tricolor	3in	yellow and blue

JUNE

	Height	Colour
Achillea millefolium	18in	white
Achillea ptarmica	2ft	white
Acorus calamus	5ft	green
Agrostemma githago	3–4ft	reddish-mauve
Anagallis arvensis	3–4in	scarlet
Anchusa officinalis	3ft	blue
Aquilegia vulgaris	2ft	navy-blue
Bellis perennis	3in	white, pink
Berberis vulgaris	2–3ft	lemon
Borago officinalis	18–20in	blue
Caltha palustris	20in	yellow
Campanula medium	2–3ft	pink, blue
Cardamine pratensis	18in	silver-blue
Centaurea cyanus	15–18in	blue
Cheiranthus cheiri	15in	orange-yellow
Chrysanthemum leucanthemum	15in	white
Convallaria majalis	8in	white
Cotoneaster microphyllus	6in	white
Cotoneaster simonsii	5ft	creamy-white
Cotyledon umbilicus	12in	greenish-white
Crataegus monogyna	10ft	white
Crataegus oxyacanthoides	8ft	cream
Cynoglossum officinale	2ft	maroon
Cytisus scoparius	8ft	yellow
Delphinium consolida	2–3ft	blue
Dianthus caesius	3–4in	pink
Dianthus caryophyllus	9in	flesh-pink
Dianthus deltoides	6–8in	dark pink
Digitalis purpurea	3ft	purple
Diplotaxis tenuifolia	18in	yellow
Drosera rotundifolia	6in	white
Dryas octopetala	4in	white
Echium vulgare	1–2ft	pink and blue
Endymion nonscriptus	15in	purple-blue
Epilobium angustifolium	3–4ft	rose-purple
Erica ciliaris	10in	white
Euphorbia virgata	18in	dull yellow
Fumaria officinalis	1–2ft	pinkish-purple

	Height	Colour
Gentiana verna	2in	blue
Geranium phaeum	18in	maroon
Geranium pratense	18in	blue
Geranium robertianum	9–12in	pink
Geranium sanguineum	12in	red
Geum rivale	12in	orange-pink
Geum urbanum	12in	yellow
Helianthemum appeninum	8in	white
Helianthemum chamaecistus	8in	yellow
Hottonia palustris	below surface	pale pink
Hypericum calycinum	15in	yellow
Hypericum humifusum	2in	yellow
Iberis amara	3–6in	white
Iris foetidissima	2ft	purple-grey
Iris pseudacorus	3ft	yellow
Leucojum aestivum	9in	white
Ligustrum vulgare	10ft	creamy-white
Lonicera caprifolium	12ft	creamy-white
Lonicera periclymenum	12ft	creamy-yellow
Lupinus arboreus	4ft	yellow
Lycopsis arvensis	9–10in	blue
Malva sylvestris	3–4ft	mauve
Menyanthes trifoliata	surface	pink and white
Mimulus guttatus	10in	yellow
Nepeta cataria	10in	mauve
Nuphar lutea	surface	yellow
Orchis morio	9in	purple
Ornithogalum pyrenaicum	2ft	green and white
Ornithogalum umbellatum	12in	white
Oxalis floribunda	8in	pink
Paeonia corallina	2ft	crimson
Papaver rhoeas	18–20in	scarlet
Papaver somniferum	2–3ft	purple
Paris quadrifolia	12in	green
Polemonium coeruleum	18in	blue
Polygonatum multiflorum	2ft	white
Polygonum bistorta	18in	pinky-red
Potentilla palustris	15in	maroon
Primula farinosa	4in	pink
Primula veris	6in	yellow
Prunus padus	10ft	white
Pyrola uniflora	6in	white
Rosa canina	8ft	pink
Rosa rubiginosa	8ft	pink
Rosa spinosissima	3ft	cream
Sagina procumbens	3in	greenish
Sagina saginoides	2in	white
Salvia horminoides	12in	blue
Salvia pratensis	2ft	purple
Sambucus nigra	20ft	creamy-white
Saxifraga aizoides	4–6in	yellow
Saxifraga hypnoides	4–6in	pinkish-white
Saxifraga stellaris	6in	white
Saxifraga umbrosa	8in	pink

	Height	Colour
Scirpus palustris	18in	brown
Scrophularia aquatica	3ft	maroon
Sedum acre	2in	yellow
Sedum album	4–6in	white
Sedum anglicum	3in	white
Sedum roseum	8in	greenish
Sedum rupestre	3in	yellow
Smyrnium olusatrum	3–4ft	yellow
Sorbus aria	20ft	cream
Sorbus aucuparia	20ft	cream
Sorbus torminalis	20ft	cream
Spiraea ulmaria	3–4ft	creamy-white
Thymus drucei	2in	purple
Thymus serpyllum	2in	rose-purple
Trollius europeus	2ft	yellow
Typha latifolia	3ft	brown
Ulex europeus	8ft	yellow
Verbascum nigrum	12–15in	yellow
Veronica tenella	3in	blue
Viburnum lantana	10ft	creamy-white
Vinca minor	9in	blue
Viola lutea	3in	yellow
Viola odorata	3in	purple
Viola tricolor	3in	yellow and blue

JULY

	Height	Colour
Achillea millefolium	18in	white
Achillea ptarmica	2ft	white
Acorus calamus	5ft	green
Agrimonia eupatoria	2ft	yellow
Agrostemma githago	3–4ft	reddish-mauve
Alyssum maritimum	3in	white
Anagallis arvensis	3–4in	scarlet
Anchusa officinalis	3ft	blue
Antirrhinum majus	16in	pink
Arbutus unedo	7ft	white
Bellis perennis	3in	white, pink
Borago officinalis	18–20in	blue
Butomus umbellatus	3–4ft	pink
Calamintha ascendens	12in	mauve-pink
Calluna vulgaris	10in	mauve
Campanula latifolia	4–5ft	blue
Campanula medium	2–3ft	pink, blue
Campanula rapunculus	2–3ft	violet
Campanula rotundifolia	8in	blue
Centaurea cyanus	15–18in	blue
Chrysanthemum leucanthemum	15in	white
Clematis vitalba	12ft	greenish-white
Cotyledon umbilicus	12in	greenish-white
Cyclamen europeum	4in	purple-red
Cynoglossum officinale	2ft	maroon
Cytisus scoparius	8ft	yellow
Delphinium consolida	2–3ft	blue
Dianthus caesius	3–4in	pink

	Height	Colour
Dianthus caryophyllus	9in	flesh pink
Dianthus deltoides	6–8in	dark pink
Diplotaxis tenuifolia	18in	yellow
Drosera rotundifolia	6in	white
Echium vulgare	1–2ft	pink and blue
Endymion nonscriptus	15in	purple-blue
Epilobium angustifolium	3–4ft	rose-purple
Epipactus helleborine	18in	yellowish-green
Erica cinera	18in	purple
Erica vagans	2–3ft	lilac pink
Eryngium maritimum	3ft	steely blue
Eupatorium cannabinum	4ft	lilac
Euphorbia virgata	18in	dull yellow
Fumaria officinalis	1–2ft	pinkish purple
Geranium pratense	18in	blue
Geranium robertianum	9–12in	pink
Geranium sanguineum	12in	red
Geum urbanum	12in	yellow
Glechoma hederacea	3in	purple
Helianthemum apenninum	8in	white
Helianthemum chamaecistus	8in	yellow
Hesperis matronalis	3ft	purple, white
Hypericum androsaemum	3ft	amber
Hypericum calycinum	15in	yellow
Hypericum hirsutum	2–3ft	yellow
Hypericum humifusum	2in	yellow
Hypericum perforatum	2–3ft	yellow
Iberis amara	3–6in	white
Impatiens biflora	3–4ft	orange
Impatiens glandulifera	4ft	mauve-pink
Inula helenium	4–5ft	yellow
Iris foetidissima	2ft	purple-grey
Iris pseudacorus	3ft	yellow
Leonurus cardiaca	4ft	mauve
Ligustrum vulgare	10ft	creamy-white
Limonium vulgare	15–18in	lavender
Lonicera caprifolium	12ft	creamy-white
Lonicera periclymenum	12ft	creamy-yellow
Lupinus arboreus	4ft	yellow
Lycopsis arvensis	9–10in	blue
Lymnanthemum nymphaeoides	surface	yellow
Lysimachia nummularia	2in	yellow
Lysimachia vulgaris	3–4ft	yellow
Lythrum salicaria	2–3ft	reddish-purple
Malva sylvestris	3–4ft	mauve
Matthiola sinuata	10–12in	purple
Metmha aquatica	3ft	reddish-purple
Minulus guttatus	10in	yellow
Myosotis alpestris	6in	blue
Nepeta cataria	10in	mauve
Nuphar lutea	surface	yellow
Nymphaea alba	surface	white
Oenothera biennis	2–3ft	yellow
Ornithogalum pyrenaicum	2ft	green and white

I

	Height	Colour
Oxalis floribunda	8in	pink
Papaver rhoeas	18–20in	scarlet
Papaver somniferum	2–3ft	purple
Peucedanum ostruthium	2ft	pink
Polemonium coeruleum	18in	blue
Polygonum bistorta	18in	pinky-red
Potentilla erecta	2ft	yellow
Pyrola minor	4in	pink
Pyrola uniflora	6in	white
Rosa arvensis	6ft	white
Rosa canina	8ft	pink
Rosa rubiginosa	8ft	pink
Rosa spinosissima	3ft	cream
Sagina nodosa	3–6in	white
Sagina procumbens	3in	greenish
Salvia horminoides	12in	blue
Salvia pratensis	2ft	purple
Sambucus nigra	20ft	creamy-white
Saponaria officinalis	2ft	pale pink
Saussurea alpine	10in	purple
Saxifraga aizoides	4–6in	yellow
Saxifraga stellaris	6in	white
Saxifraga umbrosa	8in	pink
Scabiosa arvensis	3ft	lilac
Scirpus lacustris	2–3ft	brown
Scirpus maritimus	3ft	brown
Scrophularia aquatica	3ft	maroon
Sedum acre	2in	yellow
Sedum album	4–6in	white
Sedum anglicum	3in	white
Sedum reflexum	3in	yellow
Sedum rupestre	3in	yellow
Silene acaulis	6in	rosy-red
Spiraea ulmaria	3–4ft	creamy-white
Stachys betonica	15in	rosy-mauve
Tamarix anglica	10ft	pink
Teucrium chamaedrys	8in	crimson
Teucrium scordium	8in	purple
Teucrium scorodonia	2ft	dull yellow
Thymus drucei	2in	purple
Thymus serpyllum	2in	rose-purple
Trollius europeus	2ft	yellow
Typha latifolia	3ft	brown
Ulex europeus	8ft	yellow
Valeriana officinalis	2ft	pale pink
Verbascum lychnitis	2ft	white
Verbascum nigrum	12–15in	yellow
Verbascum thapsus	5–6ft	yellow
Verbena officinalis	15in	mauve
Veronica alpina	4in	blue
Veronica tenella	3in	blue
Viburnum opulus	10ft	creamy-white
Vinca minor	9in	blue
Viola lutea	3in	yellow

	Height	Colour
Viola tricolor	3in	yellow and blue

AUGUST

	Height	Colour
Achillea millefolium	18in	white
Agrimonia eupatoria	2ft	yellow
Agrostemma githago	3–4ft	reddish-mauve
Alyssum maritimum	3in	white
Anagallis arvensis	3–4in	scarlet
Anchusa officinalis	3ft	blue
Antirrhinum majus	16in	pink
Armeria maritima	6in	pink
Borago officinalis	18–20in	blue
Butomus umbellatus	3–4ft	pink
Calamintha ascendens	12in	mauve-pink
Calluna vulgaris	10in	mauve
Campanula latifolia	4–5ft	blue
Campanula rapunculus	2–3ft	violet
Campanula rotundifolia	8in	blue
Centaurea cyanus	15–18in	blue
Chrysanthemum leucanthemum	15in	white
Clematis vitalba	12ft	greenish-white
Cotyledon umbilicus	12in	greenish-white
Cyclamen europeum	4in	purple-red
Cynoglossum officinale	2ft	maroon
Dianthus deltoides	6–8in	dark pink
Digitalis purpurea	3ft	purple
Echium vulgare	1–2ft	pink and purple
Epilobium angustifolium	3–4ft	rose-purple
Epipactis helleborine	18in	yellowish-green
Erica cinerea	18in	purple
Erica vagans	2–3ft	lilac pink
Erica vulgaris	12in	mauve
Eryngium maritimum	3ft	steely blue
Eupatorium cannabinum	4ft	lilac
Geranium sanguineum	12in	red
Geum urbanum	12in	yellow
Hesperis matronalis	3ft	purple,white
Hypericum androsaemum	3ft	amber
Hypericum calycinum	15in	yellow
Hypericum hirsutum	2–3ft	yellow
Hypericum humifusum	2in	yellow
Hypericum perforatum	2–3ft	yellow
Iberus amara	3–6in	white
Impatiens biflora	3–4ft	orange
Impatiens glandulifera	4ft	mauve-pink
Impatiens noli-tangere	2–3ft	yellow
Inula helenium	4–5ft	yellow
Iris pseudacorus	3ft	yellow
Leonurus cardiaca	4ft	mauve
Limonium binervosum	6in	lavender
Limonium vulgare	15–18in	lavender
Lonicera caprifolium	12ft	creamy-white
Lonicera periclymenum	12ft	creamy-yellow
Lycopsis arvensis	9–10in	blue

	Height	Colour
Lysimachia vulgaris	3–4ft	yellow
Lythrum salicaria	2–3ft	reddish-purple
Malva sylvestris	3–4ft	mauve
Matthiola sinuata	12–15in	purple
Mentha pulegium	4in	lilac
Mentha rotundifolia	18in	pale mauve
Mentha sylvestris	2ft	mauve
Mimulus guttatus	10in	yellow
Myosotis alpestris	6in	blue
Nuphar lutea	surface	yellow
Nymphaea alba	surface	white
Oenanthe fistulosa	15in	pink
Oenothera biennis	2–3ft	yellow
Oxalis floribunda	8in	pink
Papaver rhoeas	18–20in	scarlet
Papaver somniferum	2–3ft	purple
Peucedanum ostruthium	2ft	pink
Polygonum bistorta	18in	pinky-red
Potentilla erecta	2ft	yellow
Pyrola minor	4in	pink
Rosa arvensis	6ft	white
Sagina nodosa	3in	white
Sagina procumbens	3in	greenish
Salvia horminoides	12in	blue
Salvia pratensis	2ft	purple
Saponaria officinalis	2ft	pale pink
Saussurea alpina	10in	purple
Saxifraga aizoides	4–6in	yellow
Scabiosa arvensis	3ft	lilac
Scirpus lacustris	2–3ft	brown
Scirpus maritimus	3ft	brown
Scrophularia aquatica	3ft	maroon
Sedum anglicum	3in	white
Sedum reflexum	3in	yellow
Spiraea ulmaria	3–4ft	creamy-white
Stachys betonica	15in	rosy-mauve
Tamarix anglica	10ft	pink
Teucrium chamaedrys	8in	crimson
Teucrium scordium	8in	purple
Teucrium scorodonia	2ft	dull yelllow
Thymus drucei	2in	purple
Thymus serpyllum	2in	rose-purple
Typha latifolia	3ft	brown
Valeriana officinalis	2ft	pale pink
Verbascum lychnitis	2ft	white
Verbascum nigrum	12–15in	yellow
Verbascum thapsus	5–6ft	yellow
Verbena officinalis	15in	mauve
Veronica alpina	4in	blue
Veronica tenella	3in	blue
Viburnum opulus	10ft	creamy-white
Viola lutea	3in	yellow
Viola tricolor	3in	yellow and blue

	Height	*Colour*
SEPTEMBER		
Achillea millefolium	18in	white
Antirrhinum majus	16in	pink
Arbutus unedo	7ft	white
Armeria maritima	6in	pink
Bellis perennis	3in	white, pink
Butomus umbellatus	3–4ft	pink
Calamintha ascendens	12in	mauve-pink
Calluna vulgaris	10in	mauve
Campanula latifolia	4–5ft	blue
Campanula rapunculus	2–3ft	violet
Campanula rotundifolia	8in	blue
Colchicum autumnale	6in	rose-mauve
Crocus nudiflorus	4in	rose-purple
Cyclamen europeum	4in	purple-red
Cynoglossum officinale	2ft	maroon
Echium vulgare	1–2ft	pink and blue
Epilobium angustifolium	3–4ft	rose-purple
Erica ciliaris	10in	white
Erica vagans	2–3ft	lilac pink
Eupatorium cannabinum	4ft	lilac
Geum urbanum	12in	yellow
Hesperis matronalis	3ft	purple, white
Impatiens biflora	3–4ft	orange
Impatiens glandulifera	4ft	mauve-pink
Impatiens noli-tangere	2–3ft	yellow
Leonurus cardiaca	4ft	mauve
Limonium binervosum	6in	lavender
Limonium vulgare	15–18in	lavender
Lonicera caprifolium	12ft	creamy-white
Lonicera periclymenum	12ft	creamy-yellow
Malva sylvestris	3–4ft	mauve
Matthiola sinuata	12–15in	purple
Mentha pulegium	4in	lilac
Mentha rotundifolia	18in	pale mauve
Mimulus guttatus	10in	yellow
Nuphar lutea	surface	yellow
Oenanthe fistulosa	15in	pink
Oenothera biennis	2–3ft	yellow
Oxalis floribunda	6–8in	rose
Polygonum bistorta	18in	pinky-red
Sagina nodosa	3–6in	white
Salvia horminoides	12in	blue
Saponaria officinalis	2ft	pale pink
Saussurea alpina	10in	purple
Scabiosa arvensis	3ft	lilac
Spiraea ulmaria	3–4ft	creamy-white
Ulex europeus	8ft	yellow
Valeriana officinalis	2ft	pale pink
Verbascum thapsus	5–6ft	yellow
Vinca minor	9in	blue
OCTOBER		
Arbutus unedo	7ft	white

	Height	Colour
Bellis perennis	3in	white, pink
Campanula latifolia	4–5ft	blue
Colchicum autumnale	6in	rose-mauve
Crocus nudiflorus	4in	rose-purple
Erica vulgaris	12in	mauve
Oxalis floribunda	8in	pink
Valeriana officinalis	2ft	pale pink
Verbascum thapsus	5–6ft	yellow

NOVEMBER

Arbutus unedo	7ft	white
Bellis perennis	3in	white, pink
Colchicum autumnale	6in	rose-mauve

DECEMBER

| *Helleborus niger* | 10in | white |

GLOSSARY

ACHENE, hard one-seeded fruit

ALTERNATE, leaves arranged one after another; or where the stamens appear between the petals

ANNUAL, a plant which completes its life cycle with twelve months

AXIL, the upper angle formed by leaf and stem

AXILLARY, borne at the axils of leaf and stem

BERRY, a fruit containing seeds embedded in its juice

BIENNIAL, a plant flowering the year after that in which the seed was sown

BRACTEOLES, small bracts attached to the base of the pedicels.

BRACTS, modified leaves present on flower stalks

CALYX, the green whorl of leaf-like organs of a flower situated below the corolla

CAPITATE, growing in heads

CAPSULE, a dry, many-seeded vessel

CATKIN, flowers of one sex closely crowded together

COLUMN, a term denoting united stamens and pistils

CORDATE, heart-shaped (when describing leaves)

CORM, a flat or round stem which dies back each year, leaving behind a new corm formed by the action of the leaves

COROLLA, whorl of floral leaves known as petals

CORYMB, a raceme of flowers on pedicels which decrease in length as they approach the top of the stem, bringing them on to the same level

CORYMBOSE, in the form of a corymb

CYME, a terminal inflorescence beneath which are side branches bearing a terminal flower

DECIDUOUS, a tree or shrub losing its leaves each autumn (fall)

DIOECIOUS, plants with differently sexed flowers on different plants with stamens on one, pistils on another, as in willow

DISC, the surface from which stamens and pistils arise

ENTIRE, leaves which are neither divided nor toothed

FARINA, leaves (or petals) covered in minute hairs which gives them a downy appearance

FILAMENT, the lower stem-like part of a stamen

FLORETS, the small rayed petals of *Compositae*

FOLLICLE, an inflated one-celled carpel

GLABROUS, smooth, glossy (leaves) without surface hairs

GLANDULAR, a secreting organ, usually raised above the leaf surface

GLAUCOUS, leaves with a bluish lustre

HIRSUTE, leaves covered in long silky hairs

IMBRICATE, arranged over each other, like the scales of a leaf bud
INVOLUCRE, whorled bracts at the base of a flower

KEEL, the lower pair of leaves in pea-like flowers

LABIATE, lipped; the corolla or calyx divided into two unequal parts as with mint, lavender flowers
LANCEOLATE, lance-shaped leaves tapering at each end
LINEAR, long, narrow leaves

MONOECIOUS, stamens and pistils on separate flowers but on same plant

NODE, point on stem where leaf is produced
NUTANS, a drooping or nodding flower

OPPOSITE, leaves which are formed opposite each other on a stem

PALMATE, segments of a leaf which spread out from a central point
PAPPUS, a hairy appendage of a seed
PELLUCID, transparent; applied to dots or glands of leaves which contain essential oil
PERENNIAL, a plant of more than two years duration as primrose, marguerite
PERIANTH, the floral parts when calyx and corolla are indistinguishable
PETIOLE, lower stalk of a leaf where it joins the main stem
POLLEN, dust or grains in the anther containing the male cells to fertilise the ovules
POLLINATION, application of pollen to the stigma
PRATENSE, growing in pasture land
PUBESCENT, leaves or stems covered in close hairs or down

RACEME, stalked flowers, borne in a spike
RHIZOME, the thickened base of a stem which usually grows horizontal below ground
ROSETTE, leaves radiating from a central underground stem, sometimes overlapping to form a circle

SEGMENT, a term used for a petal of a flower or parts of a leaf divided to the mid-rib
SERRATE, tooth-edged leaves
SESSILE, stalkless, as in some leaves
SOLITARY, flowers borne singly, one to a stalk
SPIKE, a stalkless raceme
SPUR, extension of the lower part of a corolla as with aquilegia
STAMEN, male organ of a flower—filament and anther
STELLATE, star-like, radiating from the centre
STIPULE, leaf-like appendages at the base of the petioles

TOMENTOSE, silky entangled hairs

UMBEL, stalked flowers arising from one point and reaching to the same level

WHORL, flowers or leaves arranged in a circle of three or more around a stem

ACKNOWLEDGEMENTS

I wish to thank Mary McMurtrie for the delightful drawings and John Gledhill for the photographs.

My sincere thanks are also due to my editor, Miss Emma Wood, for help and advice in the preparation of this manuscript and to Doris Gatling for typing and assembling my notes on *The Wild-Flower Garden* in her usual meticulous way.

INDEX

Achillea millefolium, 30, 130
Achillea ptarmica, 30, 130
Acorus calamus, 76, 130
Agrimonia eupatoria, 29, 130
Agrimony, common, 12, 16, 29, 130
Agrimony fragrant, 12
Agrimony hemp, 26
Alexanders, 113
Allium schoenoprasum, 117
Althaea palustris, 80, 130
Anemone nemorosa, 92, 130
Anemone pulsatilla, 38, 65
Angelica, 113
Angelica archangelica, 114
Angelica sylvestris, 114
Anthemis nobilis, 117
Antirrhinum majus, 50, 130
Apium graveolens, 115
Aquilegia vulgaris, 79, 130
Arabis, 65
Arbutus unedo, 110, 130
Armeria maritima, 37, 130
Arrowhead, 74, 133
Artemesia absinthinum, 118
Artemesia vulgaris, 118
Autumn crocus, 87, 130

Bacon, Francis, 56
Balm, 120
Bardfield oxlip, 43
Basil, wild, 122
Beers, tonic, 16, 30, 120
Bellflower, giant, 24, 130
Bellis perennis, 39, 130
Berberis vulgaris, 105, 130
Bird cherry, 22, 99, 133
Bistort, 33, 133
Blackthorn, 100
Bluebell, 85, 131
Bog garden, 81; its making, 81

Bogbean, 73
Borage, 14, 16, 130
Border: its planting, 23; of wild flowers, 21; preparing the, 22
Broom, 109, 131
Buddleia davidii, 106
Burghley, Lord, 19
Bullrush: false, 74, 133; true, 74
Butomus umbellatus, 74, 130

Calamint, 56, 122
Calamintha ascendens, 56, 122
Calamintha vulgaris, 122
Calluna vulgaris, 67, 130
Caltha palustris, 75, 130
Campanula latifolia, 24, 130
Campanula medium, 25, 130
Campanula rapunculus, 24, 130
Campanula rotundifolia, 67, 130
Canterbury bell, 27, 130
Caraway, 116
Cardamine pratensis, 28, 130
Catmint, 34, 132
Cerastium alpinum, 67
Cerastium cerastoides, 67, 130
Chamomile, 16, 117
Chaucer, 40, 51
Cheddar pink, 10, 51, 131
Cheiranthus cheiri, 49, 130
Chervil, 115
Chicory, 15, 16; for forcing, 15
Chives, 117
Christmas rose, 91, 131
Clare, John, 43
Clary, 32, 133
Clematis vitalba, 103, 104
Colchicum autumnale, 86, 130
Coles, William, 16
Columbine, 79, 130
Common St John's wort, 7, 16, 105, 132

Convallaria majalis, 83, 130
Cornflower, 10
Costmary, 19
Cotoneaster microphyllus, 64, 130
Cotoneaster simonsii, 104
Cotyledon umbilicus, 52, 130
Cowslip, 8, 10, 16, 19, 41, 43, 65, 133
Crab, flowering, 22, 100
Crataegus monogyma, 100, 130
Crataegus oxyacanthoides, 100, 130
Crocus nudiflorus, 87, 130
Culpeper, 34, 56, 78, 101, 116
Cyclamen, common, 91, 130
Cyclamen, ivy-leaf, 91, 130
Cyclamen europeum, 91, 130
Cyclamen hederifolium, 91, 130
Cynoglossum officinale, 27, 131
Cytisus scoparius, 109, 131

Daffodil, wild, 59, 87
Daisy, double, 39, 59, 130
Dame's violet, 31, 131
Daphne laureola, 111
Daphne mezereum, 111
Dianthus caryophyllus, 51, 131
Dianthus causius, 51, 131
Dianthus deltoides, 52, 63, 131
Dianthus plumarius, 51, 131
Digitalis purpurea, 95, 131
Diplotaxis tenuifolia, 57
Distilled waters, 15, 24
Dog rose, 101, 133

Eglantine, 102, 133
Elder, 104
Elecampane, 10, 16, 24
Endymion nonscriptus, 85, 131
Epilobium angustifolium, 27, 131
Epilobium hirsutum, 96
Eranthus hyemalis, 84, 131
Erica ciliaris, 111, 131
Erica cinerea, 110, 131
Erica tetralix, 111, 131
Erica vagans, 110, 131
Erica vulgaris, 110, 131
Eryngium maritimum, 25, 131
Eupatorium cannabinum, 26, 131
Evelyn, John, 16, 44
Eye lotions, 15, 34

Featherfew, 37, 118
Fennel, 16, 19, 113
Fernie, Dr, 14
Forget-me-not, 10, 19, 132; alpine, 67, 132; wood, 95
Foxglove, 10, 95, 131
Fritillaria meleagris, 86, 131
Fritillary, 86, 131

Gagea lutea, 84, 131
Gentian, spring, 64, 131
Gentiana verna, 64, 131
Geranium phaeum, 32, 131
Geranium pratense, 32, 131
Geranium sanguineum, 32, 64, 131
Gerard, 13, 19, 25, 27, 31, 33, 34, 42, 46, 52, 77, 80, 85, 91, 94, 100, 103
Geum rivale, 78, 131
Geum urbanum, 12, 33, 131
Glechoma hederacea, 94, 131
Globe flower, 75, 134
Gorse, 109, 134
Grape hyacinth, 85, 132
Grieve, James, 46
Ground ivy, 94, 131

Hanmer, Sir Thomas, 28
Harebell, 67, 130
Hawkweed, purple, 34, 133
Hawthorn, 100, 130
Heartsease, 46, 134
Hedge, value of, 8
Helianthemum apenninum, 64, 131
Helianthemum chamaecistus, 64, 131
Helleborine, 96
Helleborus foetidus, 92, 131
Helleborus niger, 91, 131
Helleborus viridis, 92, 131
Herb bennet, 7, 33
Herb garden, 112; its planting, 113
Herb Paris, 94, 133
Herb Robert, 7, 131
Hesperis matronalis, 31, 131
Hill, Thomas, 83
Honeysuckle, 103, 132
Hottonia palustris, 73
Hound's tongue, 27, 131
Hypericum androsaemum, 106, 131

Hypericum calycinum, 106, 131
Hypericum perforatum, 105, 132

Iris foetidissima, 93, 132
Iris pseudacorus, 76, 132
Irish heath, 110, 131

Jacob's ladder, 32, 133
Jekyll, Gertrude, 44
John Innes Compost, 48, 124

Lady's smock, 14, 16, 28, 130
Lawrence, John, 83
Lent lily, 87, 132
Leonorus cardiaca, 26, 132
Lesser celandine, 76
Leucojum aestivum, 88, 132
Leucojum vernum, 88, 132
Ligusticum scolicum, 114, 115
Ligustrum vulgare, 106, 132
Lily-of-the-valley, 13, 15, 83, 130
Lime, caustic, 23
Limestone, 61
Limonium vulgare, 27, 66, 132
Ling, 67
Loddon lily, 88, 132
London, George, 41
London pride, 40
Lonicera caprifolium, 103, 132
Lonicera periclymenum, 103, 132
Loosestrife, purple, 79, 96
Loosestrife, yellow, 79, 96
Lovage, 114
Love-in-idleness, 45, 134
Lungwort, 33, 133
Lupinus arboreus, 109, 132
Lysimachia nummularia, 79
Lysimachia thyrsiflora, 79, 132
Lysimachia vulgaris, 79, 132
Lyte, Henry, 88
Lythrum salicaria, 79, 132

Mahonia aquifolium, 105, 132
Maiden pink, 52, 131
Mallow, common, 25
Mallow, musk, 26
Marguerite, 39
Marjoram, 37, 120
Marrubium vulgare, 120

Marsh marigold, 19, 75
Marshmallow, 15, 80
May blossom, 100, 130
Meadow crane's-bill, 32
Meadow saffron, 86, 130
Meadow sage, 33
Meadowsweet, 19, 78, 134
Melissa officinalis, 121
Mentha aquatica, 77, 132
Mentha citrata, 78, 132
Mentha piperita, 121, 132
Mentha pulegium, 77, 132
Mentha rotundifolia, 77, 121, 132
Mentha spicata, 122, 132
Mentha sylvestris, 78, 132
Milton, 49
Monkey flower, 74, 132
Motherwort, 26, 132
Mountain ash, 101, 133
Mouse-ear, 67
Mugwort, 118
Mulching, 9, 41
Mullein, 16, 24
Muscari racemosum, 85, 132
Musk rose, 102, 133
Musk stork's-bill, 7
Myrrhis odorata, 115
Myrica gale, 105, 132

Narcissus obvallaris, 88
Narcissus pseudonarcissus, 87, 88, 132
Navelwort, 52, 130
Nepeta cataria, 34, 132
Nuphar lutea, 73, 132
Nymphaea alba, 73, 132

Oenanthe fistulosa, 76, 132
Orchis maculata, 96
Orchis morio, 96, 132
Origanum vulgare, 120
Ornithogalum nutans, 84, 132
Ornithogalum pyrenaicum, 84
Ornithogalum umbellatum, 84, 132
Oxalis floribunda, 34, 64, 132
Oxalis, pink, 34, 64, 132
Oxlip, 41, 43, 133
Oxlip, false, 44

Paeonia corallina, 29

Pansy, 45, 134
Paris quadrifolia, 94, 133
Parkinson, 28, 33, 46, 50, 55, 84, 116
Parsley, 117
Pasque-flower, 38, 65, 133
Path, its making, 58
Pearl-wort, alpine, 65, 133
Pearl-wort, knotted, 57, 65, 133
Pechey, John, 14, 30
Pennycress, 65
Pennyroyal, 16, 19, 77
Peony, 29, 133
Peppermint, 16, 121
Periwinkle, lesser, 40, 134
Phillips, Henry, 50, 88
Pinks, 51, 59
Polemonium coeruleum, 32, 133
Polygonatum multiflorum, 83, 133
Polygonum bistorta, 33, 133
Pool: making, 72; planting, 73
Potentilla erecta, 103, 133
Potentilla palustris, 80, 133
Poterium sanquisorba, 116
Primrose, 8, 13, 41, 65, 133; birds-eye,
    65, 133; double, 41; hose-in-hose,
    41; Jack-in-green, 42; propagation,
    42
Primula elatior, 43, 133
Primula farinosa, 61, 65, 133
Primula veris, 41, 133
Primula vulgaris, 41, 133
Privet, common, 106, 132
Propagation: by division, 126; from
    cuttings, 128
Prunella vulgaris, 57
Prunus cerasifera, 101
Prunus padus, 22, 99, 133
Prunus spinosa, 100
Pulmonaria officinalis, 33, 133
Pulsatilla vulgaris, 38, 65, 133
Purslane, 13
Pyrola minor, 67, 133
Pyrola uniflora, 67, 133

Rampion, 24, 130
Rea, John, 44
Roast beef plant, 93, 132
Robinson, Wm, 93

Rock garden: its making, 61; plants
    for a, 63
Rock rose, 64, 131
Rock spray, 64, 130
Rosa arvensis, 102, 133
Rosa canina, 101, 133
Rosa rubiginosa, 102, 133
Rosa spinosissima, 102
Rose-root, 19, 133
Rosebay, 27, 131
Rush, flowering, 74, 130

Sagina nodosa, 57, 65, 133
Sagina procumbens, 57, 133
Sagina saginoides, 65, 133
Sagittaria sagitifolia, 74, 133
Salad burnet, 7, 12, 116
Salads, herbs for, 13, 43
Salvia horminoides, 32, 133
Salvia pratensis, 33, 133
Sandstone, 62
Saponaria officinalis, 28, 63, 133
Saussurea alpina, 34, 133
Saxifraga aizoides, 55, 66, 133
Saxifraga hypnoides, 55, 66, 133
Saxifraga oppositifolia, 66, 133
Saxifraga stellaris, 65, 133
Saxifraga umbrosa, 40, 133
Saxifrage, 55, 133; golden, 55, 133;
    mossy, 66, 133; purple, 66, 133;
    starry, 65, 133
Scabiosa arvensis, 31, 133
Scented waters, 19
Scilla verna, 59, 63, 91
Scirpus lacustris, 74, 133
Scott, Sir Walter, 50
Sea holly, 25, 131
Sea lavender, 27, 66, 132
Sedum acre, 48, 52, 64, 133
Sedum album, 55, 64, 133
Sedum reflexum, 64
Sedum roseum, 19, 133
Sedum rupestre, 52, 133
Seed: its harvesting, 10, 123; sowing,
    124
Service tree, 101, 134
Shakespeare, 14, 41, 43, 44, 45, 56, 87,
    100, 102
Shrub border, 97; plants for, 100

Silene acaulis, 66, 133
Snapdragon, 50, 130
Sneezewort, 30, 130
Snowdrop, 59, 88
Soapwort, 27, 63, 133
Soil, its preparation, 22, 41, 98
Solomon's seal, 83, 133
Sorbus aria, 101, 133
Sorbus aucuparia, 101, 133
Sorbus terminalis, 101
Speedwell, alpine, 67
Spinney, plants for, 82
Spiraea ulmaria, 78, 134
Spring snowflake, 88, 132
Stachys betonica, 31, 134
Star of Bethlehem, 84, 131
Stonecrop, 48, 52, 64, 133
Strewing plants, 19
Sweet alyssum, 57, 130
Sweet amber, 7, 106
Sweet briar, 102, 133
Sweet flag, 19, 76, 130
Sweet gale, 105, 132
Sweet rocket, 13, 31, 131
Sweet scabious, 31

Tamarix anglica, 109, 134
Tanacetum vulgare, 119
Tansy, 16, 19, 119
Teas, tonic, 16, 30, 118, 120
Teucrium chamaedrys, 55, 134
Teucrium scordium, 76
Teucrium scorodonia, 94
Thrift, 37, 130
Thlaspi alpestre, 65, 134
Thyme, wild, 56, 59, 121, 134
Thymus drucei, 56, 121, 134
Thymus serpyllum, 56, 134
Tradescant, John, 44
Tree lupin, 109, 132
Trollius europeus, 75, 134
Trough, 58; making a, 59
Tulipa sylvestris, 83, 134
Tusser, Thomas, 15, 19, 44, 55
Typha latifolia, 74, 134

Ulex europeus, 109, 134

Valerian, 50, 134
Valeriana officinalis, 50, 134
Verbascum thapsus, 24, 134
Verbena officinalis, 34, 134
Veronica alpina, 67, 134
Vervain, 34, 134
Viburnum lantana, 104, 134
Viburnum opulus, 104, 134
Victoria, Queen, 45
Vinca minor, 40, 134
Viola canina, 45
Viola lutea, 46
Viola odorata, 44, 134
Viola tricolor, 45, 134
Violet, 13, 44; its culture, 45; its
  perfume, 45

Wall: making a, 48; planting a, 48;
  plants for a, 47, 49
Wall germander, 55, 134
Wall rocket, 57
Wallflower, 7, 49, 130; its culture, 50
Water dropwort, 76
Water figwort, 77
Water garden, 69
Water germander, 76
Water iris, 76
Water lily, 73
Water mint, 77, 132
Wild flowers: planting, 126; propaga-
  tion, 126, 129
Wild plants for bedding, 37
Wild Plants Protection Act, 10
Wild rose, 101, 133
Wild tulip, 83, 134
Willow herb, 27, 96
Winter aconite, 84, 131
Wintergreen, 67
Wood anemone, 92, 130
Wood avens, 12, 78
Wood betony, 31, 134
Wood sage, 94
Wood spurge, 93
Wordsworth, 76
Wormwood, 118

Yarrow, 30, 130